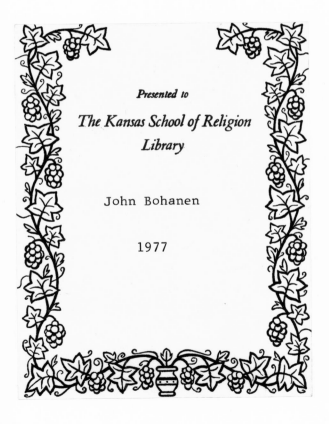

The Poetry of Civic Virtue

The Poetry of Civic Virtue

ELIOT • MALRAUX • AUDEN

by
Nathan A. Scott, Jr.

FORTRESS PRESS   Philadelphia

Also by Nathan A. Scott, Jr.
Rehearsals of Discomposure: Alienation and Reconciliation in Modern Literature (1952)
Modern Literature and the Religious Frontier (1958)
Albert Camus (1962)
Reinhold Niebuhr (1963)
Samuel Beckett (1965)
The Broken Center: Studies in the Theological Horizon of Modern Literature (1966)
Ernest Hemingway (1966)
Craters of the Spirit: Studies in the Modern Novel (1968)
Negative Capability: Studies in the New Literature and the Religious Situation (1969)
The Unquiet Vision: Mirrors of Man in Existentialism (1969)
Nathanael West (1971)
The Wild Prayer of Longing: Poetry and the Sacred (1971)
Three American Moralists—Mailer, Bellow, Trilling (1973)

Edited by Nathan A. Scott, Jr.
The Tragic Vision and the Christian Faith (1957)
The New Orpheus: Essays toward a Christian Poetic (1964)
The Climate of Faith in Modern Literature (1964)
Man in the Modern Theatre (1965)
Four Ways of Modern Poetry (1965)
Forms of Extremity in the Modern Novel (1965)
The Modern Vision of Death (1967)
Adversity and Grace: Studies in Recent American Literature (1968)
The Legacy of Reinhold Niebuhr (1975)

1. Literature and Society

Excerpts from *Four Quartets* by T. S. Eliot are reprinted by permission of Harcourt Brace Jovanovich, Inc.; copyright, 1973, by T. S. Eliot; copyright, 1971, by Esme Valerie Eliot.

Library of Congress Catalog Card Number 76–007871
ISBN 0–8006–0483–0

5783E76   Printed in U.S.A.   1-483

Contents

To
Anthony, Priscilla, and Christopher Yu

Preface

The organizing theme of this book, as it bears upon the virtues
proper to the City and how they have been conceived in certain
exemplary texts of our time, does not make any primary reference to the issues of sociology, however much they may of
necessity be felt to hover in the background. The various ways
in which the literary imagination has responded to the actual
phenomenon of the modern city have, of course, been lately
studied by a host of writers—most brilliantly perhaps by Donald
Fanger,[1] Irving Howe,[2] and Raymond Williams.[3] And these re-
searches have well established how regularly in modern literature—from Balzac and Dickens and Dostoevsky to Ellison and
Bellow and Lowell—the metropolis has been regarded as crush-
ingly and absolutely *against* the human venture. In his poem
of 1819, "Peter Bell the Third," Shelley declared that "Hell is a
city much like London—/A populous and a smoky city. . . ."
And it is a shudder not unlike Shelley's that we hear in *Les
Fleurs du Mal*—before the *fourmillante cité* of Baudelaire's
Paris, in *The Trial*—before the labyrinthine chaos of Kafka's
Prague, in *Auto-da-fé*—before the phantasmagoric underworld
of Elias Canetti's Vienna, or in *Invisible Man*—before the terrible shiftiness of life in Ellison's New York. The urban scene
—by Gogol, Flaubert, Conrad, Joyce, Céline, Dreiser, Alfred
Döblin, Brecht—is thought to be a place of slums and sickness,
of bedlam and treachery, of loneliness and dereliction; and,
whether it be St. Petersburg or Dublin or Chicago or Berlin, it
is supposed (as Poe says in "The City in the Sea") that "No

1. See Donald Fanger, *Dostoevsky and Romantic Realism* (Cambridge:
Harvard University Press, 1965).
2. See Irving Howe, "The City in Literature," in *The Critical Point* (New
York: Horizon Press, 1973), pp. 39–58.
3. See Raymond Williams, *The Country and the City* (London: Chatto
and Windus, 1973).

rays from the holy heaven come down/On the long night-time of that town."

This now familiar revulsion of modern literary sensibility by the social actualities of metropolitan life touches my theme, however, only in the degree to which it is the one side of a coin the other side of which is the discreditation of authority that our literature records with respect to the ancient claim of *communitas* to be the great limiting and fulfilling condition of human existence. And the one fact is surely not unrelated to the other. For when the ordinary, outer world—which is, of course, in the modern period predominantly urban—appears, despite its flurry and bustle, to be something like a wilderness and when the public sector of life is felt to be (in Kierkegaard's definition) merely "a kind of gigantic something, an abstract and deserted void which is everything and nothing,"[4] then the impulse to embrace the "universe within" is likely to prove well-nigh irresistible.

Indeed, the late Georg Lukács, more insistently perhaps than any other major critic of the recent past, maintained that the withdrawal of allegiance to the idea of man-in-society is that which, above all else, distinguishes "the ideology of modernism" in literature. For, as he looked at the great protagonists of the modern movement, it seemed that most of them—Gide, Kafka, Musil, Beckett, to mention only a few of his exemplars—represented a very profound skepticism about the possibility of the public world of social engagements affording any viable context for the life of human selfhood. Lukács took it for granted that man is by nature a social creature, the *zoon politikon*, but he was persuaded that "the ontology on which the image of man in modernist literature is based invalidates this principle,"[5] since it generally posits a radical solitariness as the universal human condition. In his analysis—and his indebtedness to Hegel is not imperceptible—the abandonment of confidence in the social world as the repository of man's essential truth inevitably leads

4. Søren Kierkegaard, *The Present Age*, trans. Alexander Dru and Walter Lowrie (London: Oxford University Press, 1940), p. 41.
5. Georg Lukács, *Realism in Our Time*, trans. John and Necke Mander (New York: Harper and Row, Harper Torchbooks, 1971), p. 24.

the human spirit to seek "its truth by retracing its steps from the external back into its own internality, leaving the outer world as an inadequate form of existence";[6] and the inwardness of individualist subjectivity thus attains a privileged status. We are conceived to be " 'thrown-into-the-world': meaninglessly, unfathomably."[7] But it is assumed that nothing much can come of our dealings with the world, since "real life" is *elsewhere*. And though "Joyce uses Dublin, Kafka and Musil the Hapsburg Monarchy, as the locus of their masterpieces," "the locus they . . . depict is little more than a backdrop [which] . . . is not basic to their artistic intention."[8] For the real locus of the authentic life is that domain which Rilke called *Weltinnenraum*[9] —inner-world-space, or world space interiorized—where the autonomous imagination of the Single One may enjoy such an unqualified sovereignty as the protagonist of Musil's *The Man without Qualities* hankers after when, in answer to the question as to what he would do if he were God, he says: "I should be compelled to abolish reality." "Subjective existence 'without qualities':"[10] this, indeed, says Lukács, is the kind of angelism by which the literary imagination in the modern period has often been mesmerized. So, as he argues, it is no wonder that the great, characteristic monuments in the literature of this century —*The Counterfeiters*, *The Castle*, *To the Lighthouse*, *Waiting for Godot*—have a strangely spectral, ghostlike quality, for they have not fed and fattened on the concrete, palpable circumstantiality of the human world: they have not been patterned after those primary forms of sociality and interdependence that define our true *Lebenswelt*, because they are actuated by "an essentially subjective vision [which] is identified with reality itself."[11]

Now Lukács's genuine greatness as a critic was something about which he himself, one feels, was never in any doubt, for

6. Georg Friedrich Wilhelm Hegel, *Aesthetik*, ed. Friedrich Bassenge (Berlin: Aufbau-Verlag, 1955), p. 496.
7. Lukács, *Realism in Our Time*, p. 21.
8. Ibid.
9. Rainer Maria Rilke, *Sämtliche Werke*, vol. 2 (Wiesbaden: Insel-Verlag, 1957), p. 93.
10. Lukács, *Realism in Our Time*, p. 25.
11. Ibid., p. 52.

his tone is always peremptory and dogmatic—to the point indeed of frequently inviting severe rejoinders, particularly with respect to his judgments of individual texts. But those who enjoy the extraordinary range of his learning and (in George Steiner's phrase) the "supreme seriousness"[12] with which he takes *écriture* will perhaps be inclined towards a certain leniency in regard to those details of his vast, multi-volume achievement that are felt to be questionable. In any event, my own citation of his testimony here is prompted not by a desire to endorse the full program of his "dialectical" method but, rather, by the coincidence between my own sense and his of what has been the general slant and emphasis represented by the "canonical" literature of the modern period. For it is precisely the short shrift which this literature has given the social idea, the idea of man-in-society, the fact of our being irrefragably "members one of another"—it is its general failure to be fascinated with the fact that the human world is most essentially an affair of what Martin Buber called the *inter*human,"[13] it is just this which has impelled me in turn to want to hold up a few large examples of *another* way, of another style of imagination, which takes the world of men to be a world of coexistence, of Coinherence, or a world of what I call (after Charles Williams) the City.

The opening chapter—which finds its *motiv* in Eliot—forms the real introduction to the "argument" underlying the pages that follow, and I need not here offer any synopsis of what it sets forth. It is sufficient now merely to say that it is, indeed, in Eliot, and in Malraux and in Auden, that I locate exemplary instances of the literary imagination supervising its project in such a way as to make it convey not some word about "a world elsewhere" but rather what Henry James called "the ache of the actual," the very form and body and pressure of that unexclusive mutuality which belongs to the true life of the City. Each of my subjects is a magnificent rhetorician, and each chooses for his text not "the huddled warmth of crowds" but (as Auden

12. George Steiner, "Georg Lukács—A Preface," in Lukács *Realism in Our Time*, p. 15.
13. See Martin Buber, *The Knowledge of Man*, trans, Maurice Friedman and Ronald Gregor Smith (New York: Harper and Row, 1965), chap. III.

phrases it) "That real republic which must be/The State all politicians claim,/Even the worst, to be their aim." So I exhibit them as poets—Malraux, too, since, as I argue, his fiction is essentially a poetic enterprise—as poets whose special distinction it is, in our own late, bad time, to prompt reflection on the nature of civic virtue. There are, of course, others to whom I might have turned, chiefest among them perhaps being William Carlos Williams; but these three (Eliot, Malraux, and Auden) will suffice, in their power to state a kind of case—that "no man is an island," that the vocation of literature is to celebrate not the various and sundry commissars who tyrannize us but the City which they betray.

In a book (*The Ordinary Universe*) bearing in its basic intentions certain similarities to my own modest effort in these essays, the Irish critic Denis Donoghue says in the opening line of the chapter entitled "Conclusion," "There is none"[14]—for, as the subtitle of the book announces, he is after nothing more than "Soundings in Modern Literature." And so it is here also—soundings in the literature of this century that speaks of how "love illuminates . . ./The city and the lion's den,/The world's great rage, the travel of young men."

I am grateful to many old friends at the University of Chicago and elsewhere the naming of whom might be embarrassing for them but without whose rallying support and kindly criticism my labors would proceed far more uncertainly. And most especially do I want to speak my thanks to the Committee on the William Belden Noble Lectures at Harvard University which, in offering me in March of 1976 the distinguished platform afforded by this lectureship, provided the occasion for which the material of my third chapter was prepared. Nor, despite my having recently joined the faculty of the University of Virginia, should I forget to salute my friend Joseph Kitagawa, the Dean of the University of Chicago's Divinity faculty, whose thoughtful generousness smoothed my way over many years and helped to make Swift Hall a place on the Chicago campus in which it was good to be.

14. Denis Donoghue, *The Ordinary Universe: Soundings in Modern Literature* (London: Faber and Faber, 1968), p. 309.

1.

The Polis *as "Time's Covenant"—* *in Eliot's Late Poetry*

Gesang ist Dasein.

—Rainer Maria Rilke

The poetry does not matter.

—T. S. Eliot

What life have you if you have not life together?
There is no life that is not in community. . . .

—T. S. Eliot

The German martyr of 1945, Dietrich Bonhoeffer, is not today
the powerfully influential presence in theology that he was in the
two decades that came to a close at the end of the 1960s. Yet
the pressure of the legacy preserved in his *Letters and Papers*
from Prison is still deeply felt, most especially in the mandate
that Bonhoeffer laid upon his contemporaries to search for "a
non-religious way" of conceiving the ultimate pattern of life and
for a new method of speaking "in secular fashion of God."[1]
Indeed, the impulse that is almost everywhere controlling the
theological imagination in our period is one that prompts a very
profound reformation of religious sensibility—in the direction of
a relinquishment of all those supernaturalist postulates of classical theism that have tended in effect to locate human existence
at a point of intersection between the two spheres of Nature
and Supernature. The whole framework of the *theologia peren-*
nis, it would seem, has at last been quite thoroughly emptied of
cogency, and its grammar is no longer felt to be conformable

1. Dietrich Bonhoeffer, *Letters and Papers from Prison*, ed. Eberhard
Bethge, trans. Reginald H. Fuller (London: Collins, Fontana Books, 1959),
pp. 124, 92.

1

with the natural assumptions of modern intelligence—which give us no good reason for supposing the universe to have a second story or some "realm . . . over and above or behind the processes of nature and history which perforates this world or breaks it by supranatural intervention."[2]

Fundamental reflection on human experience does, of course, still entail, inevitably, the pondering of questions that are of an essentially religious order. For men today, no less than in any previous time, seek assurances that ours is a world charged with "a kind of total grandeur at the end,"[3] tabernacling grace and glory and thus open to sacramental appropriation. But when they do feel themselves impelled to make something like the ultimate affirmation of religious faith—that the world is *for* us rather than *against* us—they no longer generally find it needful or possible to express this confidence by way of any invocation of a divine *Pantokrator* or of a God-thing to whose "existence" (up above, in the skies) that of all other beings is subordinate. The established canons of modern thought tell us that we dwell in *one* world rather than at a point of intersection between two: we can no longer make room in the mind for any transcenden-tally spatialized personal entity belonging to some *terra incognita* "above" or "beyond" our world, and the God of (as Heidegger would say) "onto-theology" is at best nothing more now than "the last fading smile of a cosmic Cheshire Cat."[4]

In his poem called "The Poet's Vocation," Friedrich Hölderlin suggests, however (in a passage on which Martin Heidegger has meditated deeply),[5] that there are times "when God's failure helps." Or, we may say that the eclipse of God may on occasion prepare the kind of exigency that provides the religious imagina-tion the possibility and the promise—if it submits to the requisite travail—of genuinely new redintegration; and it is conceivable

2. John A. T. Robinson, *Exploration into God* (Stanford: Stanford University Press, 1967), p. 80.
3. Wallace Stevens, "To an Old Philosopher in Rome," in *The Collected Poems of Wallace Stevens* (New York: Alfred A. Knopf, 1955), p. 510.
4. Julian Huxley, *Religion without Revelation* (London: Max Parrish, 1957), p. 58.
5. Martin Heidegger, "Remembrance of the Poet," trans. Douglas Scott, in *Existence and Being* (Chicago: Henry Regnery Co., 1949), pp. 286–90.

that the arrival of such a moment is presently signalized by the extraordinary experimentation and revisionism that are so notably a part of contemporary theology. The categories of "absolute theism"[6] and the metaphysical entailments of traditional super-naturalist piety represent, in the figure Bishop Robinson was employing a decade ago, a currency no longer negotiable: the "area of exchange" within which it was once accepted and could therefore be floated has well-nigh disappeared: its "backing" or "cash value" is no longer taken for granted—and the resulting currency crisis is so radical as to make futile any mere attempt at strengthening the purchasing power of the old money by internal reforms: it simply has to be replaced by a new currency.[7] Or, again, in Amos Wilder's pungent formulation:

> If we are to have any transcendence today . . . it must be in and through the secular. If we are to have any mystery it must be the lay mystery. If we are to find Grace it is to be found in the world and not overhead. The sublime firmament of over-head reality . . . has collapsed.[8]

So fresh moorings are being sought, and it is in this quest that very nearly everywhere—amongst theologians of the Reformation line as well as of Catholic Christianity—the religious enterprise is to be found engaged.

Now it is not unnatural that in such a period a principal effort of theology should come to be what it now is—namely, that of attempting to take a "step behind" the incrustations of its own funded tradition, in order that it may "retrieve" that primitive enthrallment by the luminous mystery of Being in which it originated. For, as it is felt, only in this way can theology once again become a truly "foundational" discipline, by seeking humbly and obediently to hearken to that—anciently spoken of as the Logos—which assembles and sustains all things: it must step backward, beyond its own hardened protocols, in order

6. The term is Leslie Dewart's: see his *The Future of Belief* (New York: Herder and Herder, 1966), pp. 64–69.

7. John A. T. Robinson, "The Debate Continues," in *The Honest to God Debate*, ed. David L. Edwards (Philadelphia: Westminster Press, 1963), pp. 243–46.

8. Amos N. Wilder, "Art and Theological Meaning," in *The New Orpheus: Essays toward a Christian Poetic*, ed. Nathan A. Scott, Jr. (New York: Sheed and Ward, 1964), pp. 407–8.

once again, forwardly, to "step barefoot into reality."[9]   And so proceeding, says the gifted theologian Heinrich Ott, the religious imagination may once more "enter 'into the freedom of saying what is entrusted to it' "[10] and thus recover its native authenticity.

In its intention to bypass the objectifying approaches of metaphysical theology to the experience of Transcendence and in its concern to recover that primal sense of wonder which gives birth to theological reflection, the stratagem that is here in view wants, of course, to reinstate the traditional kinship between poetry and religion.   For if, as it were, the initiative is once again to be accorded to the mysterious fecundity of Being and if language is that which lets Being "appear," if the poet is he who more than any other is adept in so supervising language as to make it transparent before the fullness of Being and if, therefore, Being is by way of coming to light in the poetic word, then the poet's response to primal reality presents us with a crucial instance of the kind of thinking that is indeed "foundational."   And thus it is not surprising that, in many circles of contemporary theology, Martin Heidegger's account of *poiesis* as the essential agency of primary truth should have taken on the immense prestige that it now holds.[11]

9. Wallace Stevens, "Large Red Man Reading," in *The Collected Poems,* p. 423.

10. Heinrich Ott, "What Is Systematic Theology?" in *The Later Heidegger and Theology,* ed. James M. Robinson and John B. Cobb, Jr. (New York: Harper and Row, 1963), p. 110.   Professor Ott is here quoting from a letter he received from Martin Heidegger on the appearance of the former's book *Denken und Sein: Der Weg Martin Heideggers und der Weg der Theologie* (Zürich: EVZ–Verlag, 1959).

11. As fairly representative expressions of the significance presently accorded this aspect of Heidegger's thought in the American theological community, one may cite such texts as the following—Robert W. Funk, *Language, Hermeneutic, and Word of God* (New York: Harper and Row, 1966); James M. Robinson and John B. Cobb, Jr., eds., *The Later Heidegger and Theology* (New York: Harper and Row, 1963); Paul J. Achtemeier, *An Introduction to the New Hermeneutic* (Philadelphia: Westminster Press, 1969); Nathan A. Scott, Jr., *Negative Capability: Studies in the New Literature and the Religious Situation* (New Haven: Yale University Press, 1969), chap. IV; Nathan A. Scott, Jr., *The Wild Prayer of Longing: Poetry and the Sacred* (New Haven: Yale University Press, 1971), chap. II; and Stanley R. Hopper and David L. Miller, eds., *Interpretation: The Poetry of Meaning* (New York: Harcourt, Brace & World, Harbinger Books, 1967). Heidegger's conception of *poiesis* as an agency of primary truth may also be felt to be very much a part of the background of Ray L. Hart's *Unfinished Man and the Imagination* (New York: Herder and Herder, 1968).

Heidegger will doubtless first of all be thought of not as a theorist of literature but as a specialist in metaphysical philosophy, as indeed perhaps the last great metaphysician of the modern period. Yet an interesting distinction of his writings of the past thirty years consists in the altogether decisive role they assign to poetic art in the reinstatement for modern consciousness of a genuinely metaphysical sensibility.[12] And no progress can be made in the appropriation of his remarkable testimony until his method for the reestablishment of foundational thinking is seen to entail a certain critique of modern culture which itself in turn leads into a certain theory of poetry.

Indeed, Heidegger considers any truly fundamental act of reflection to be an affair of "poetizing,"[13] for it is the poet (*der Dichter*) who is, in his view, far more than the thinker (*der Denker*), a proficient in the art of "paying heed" to the things of earth. And it is just the capacity for this kind of attentiveness that he regards as the great casualty of those attitudes toward the world engendered by a culture so heavily dominated as our own by the general outlook of scientific positivism. For, in such a climate, the sovereign passion controlling all transactions with reality is that of turning everything to practical account: the furniture of the world is approached predatorily, with an intention to manipulate it and convert it to use. And, inevitably, as a consequence, a certain "godlessness" enters into the texture of human experience. Which is to say that, when the only glance regularly bestowed on the world is that of "calculative thinking"[14] and when our principal concern is that of simply making it obedient to an enterprise of science or engineering, a very profound impoverishment of sensibility ensues. For to

12. Heidegger's theory of poetry finds its most significant statement in two focal texts: the *Interpretations of Hölderlin's Poetry—Erläuterungen zu Hölderlins Dichtung* (Frankfurt-am-Main: Vittorio Klostermann, 1944); and the book called *Paths in the Forest—Holzwege* (Frankfurt-am-Main: Vittorio Klostermann, 1950). Also, Albert Hofstadter has assembled and translated into English a superb collection of the writings on poetry—Martin Heidegger, *Poetry, Language, Thought* (New York: Harper and Row, 1971).

13. Heidegger, *Holzwege*, p. 303.

14. See Martin Heidegger, "Memorial Address," *passim*, in *Discourse on Thinking*, trans. John M. Anderson and E. Hans Freund (New York: Harper and Row, 1966), pp. 43–57.

have abdicated from any intimate relationship with the things and creatures of earth, to be utterly mesmerized by our own grasping, manipulative purposes, is to have lost any capacity for reverential awe before the sheer ontological weight and depth of the world—and is thus to be alienated from that in relation to which alone human selfhood can be securely constituted. What is lost is just any lively sense of the intransigent otherness in the various concrete givens of experience, any real appreciation of the stoutness and stubbornness with which they persist in retaining a specificity that will not be blotted out by our human intentionality. And to have lost this special kind of percipience is to be under the sway of godlessness: it is to be without knowledge of the Holy (*das Heilige*), of the radically immanent presence of Being within the things of earth, that primal energy which gathers things into themselves and which is the Source (*Ursprung*) not only of the externalities by which we are surrounded but of ourselves as well.

But now it is the testimony of this last great systematician of modern philosophy that it is on poetry rather than philosophy that we must count for the liberation of human intelligence from its "forgetfulness" of Being. For it is the poet who presses a relentless kind of quest for intimacy of relationship with the various particular realities of experience, not with the "light that never was on land or sea" but with the concrete actualities of the world, with the unique historical event, with the unrepeatable personal encounter, with all the rich singularity that belongs to "things" in their intractable specificity. The poet is, of course, constantly handling similes and metaphors and epithets, and often in an elaborately measured language. But he works most essentially with imagery, with words highly charged with the kind of emotivity that posits brilliantly sensuous pictures of the world. And what the image wants to do is to interrupt the normally routinized procedures of consciousness by way of initiating some fresh engagement between the imagination and the salient, palpable immediacies of lived experience. It is the greenness of *this* grass, the poignancy of the separation of *these* lovers, the "moonlit dome" of *this* man's dream, that the poetic word seeks to bring into the light of cleansed and intensified awareness. So, thinking most especially of Hölderlin and Rilke, whom he takes as his exemplary models, Heidegger says: "The poet names the gods"—which is to say that he "names all things in that which they are,"[15] "so that things for the first time shine out. . . ."[16] By approaching them not with any practical or manipulative purpose but only with an intention to give heed to the bright actuality of their concrete presence, the poet directs our attention to the enduring powers (the "gods") whereby the things of earth are enabled simply to be what they are. And thus the miracle that happens in the work of art, as Heidegger says in the famous opening essay of the *Holzwege* ("Der Ursprung des Kunstwerkes"), is "the letting happen of the advent of the truth of what is. . . ."[17] In short, the poem puts us in mind of that wherewith things are inwardly constituted, of that by which they are so assembled as to enable them to stand out before the gaze of the mind—and, insofar as the poem does this, it brings us into the region of that-which-is: it "deconceals" the things of this world, brings them "into the Open," and thus brings us into the neighborhood of Being. So "truth is at work"[18] in poetic art, since it is nothing less than the "voice" of Being.

Indeed, as Heidegger insists again and again, the kind of response which is made to the affairs of life by the poet presents the highest measure of how the generality of men must sojourn in the world, if in fact they are truly to have a "world." For it is only when we consent to deal with the things of earth in the spirit of what he calls *Gelassenheit* (that is, acquiescence, surrender, abandonment), it is only when we give up the urge to exploit and master them and approach them in the marveling, reverential spirit of "paying heed" and "letting-be"[19]—it is only then that we may be granted that "releasement"[20] toward them

15. Martin Heidegger, "Hölderlin and the Essence of Poetry," trans. Douglas Scott, in *Existence and Being*, p. 304.

16. Ibid., p. 305.

17. The quotation is from Albert Hofstadter's translation of the essay ("The Origin of the Work of Art") in *Poetry, Language, Thought*, p. 72.

18. Ibid., *passim.*

19. Martin Heidegger, "On the Essence of Truth," trans. R. F. C. Hull and Alan Crick, in *Existence and Being*, pp. 319–51.

20. Heidegger, *Discourse on Thinking*, pp. 54–55.

which permits Being to come forth and be manifest. Which is, of course, just what the poetic word accomplishes: by the very gentleness with which it lets things be, by the rapt attentiveness toward their radiant actuality which it solicits, it summons forth and lights up that by which they are gathered into themselves and which is nothing other than Being itself. And to have come into the region of that-which-is is to dwell no longer amid the "concealments" and ambiguity of earth but amid Openness (*Offenheit*) and the Non-concealed (*das Unverborgene*): it is in truth to have at last a "world." Or, we may say that the poetic word is precisely that which lets the earth become a world, insofar as it "clears" the earth and releases the things of earth from their "self-seclusion" and concealment (*Vorborgenheit*), thus enabling them to "know" one another and to form a unified matrix of meanings and relations whereby the human spirit may be upborne.[21] Hence, as Heidegger concludes (by way of his meditations on a late poem by Hölderlin),[22] it is "poetically [that] man dwells on this earth," insofar as he manages to dwell at all in a truly human way. For to be fully human is to have a world, and man is granted a world only in the measure to which the things of earth are brought out of darkness and into the Open—and this transformation of "earth" into "world" (the "event of Being") is accomplished by the poetic word.

"Language," says Heidegger, "is the house of being"[23]—by which he means that it is only through the instrumentality of the word that reality may be rescued from oblivion. The task of the word is to "name" the things of earth, but this naming is not merely an affair of handing out titles: it is, rather, a matter of bringing "the presence of what was previously uncalled into a nearness."[24] To name a creature or an event is to release it from

21. See Heidegger, "The Origin of the Work of Art" in *Poetry, Language, Thought*, pp. 39–57.
22. See Heidegger, "Hölderlin and the Essence of Poetry" in *Existence and Being* and "'. . . Poetically Man Dwells . . .'" in *Poetry, Language, Thought*.
23. Martin Heidegger, *Unterwegs zur Sprache* (Pfullingen: Neske Verlag, 1960), p. 166.
24. Heidegger, *Poetry, Language, Thought*, p. 198.

the undifferentiated obscurity of existence and to summon it forth into the light of its own actuality. The word does in truth allow things to be, and thus they may be said to have their abode in language. Indeed, as Heidegger maintains, "Language is not a mere tool . . . which man possesses; on the contrary, it is only language that affords the very possibility of standing in the openness of the existent. Only where there is language, is there world. . . ."[25] But since it is precisely poetic speech which constitutes the quintessential instance of authentic language, his thought does in effect finally line itself up behind the radical proposition that it is poetry which is the house of Being, that it is the poet who is the guardian or the "shepherd of Being,"[26] and that it is he who gives us a world in which to dwell.

Now the conception of the poet's task which Martin Heidegger advances is one that conforms very exactly with the mission undertaken in a central line of poetry since the the close of the eighteenth century. For, as Walter Strauss was recently reminding us in one of the profoundest accounts of modern literature produced by the scholarship of our period,[27] the name of many of the focal poets from Novalis to Mallarmé and Valéry and from Blake to Rilke and St.-John Perse has been that of the ancient Thracian lyrist—called Orpheus—who (as Ovid relates in *The Metamorphoses*, bks. X and XI), when he touched his frail golden lyre, brought all lads and lasses, birds and beasts, even the stones and trees, under his spell. This "seer and bard in one," says Horace, "weaned savage forest-tribes from murder and foul living,"[28] and the extraordinary capacity of his music to bring order and peace to the earth won him so hallowed a place in the lore of Latin antiquity that, mythical figure though he was, across all the ages of Western history he has remained the very type and example of the poet as shaman and theurgist, as

25. Heidegger, "Hölderlin and the Essence of Poetry," in *Existence and Being*, pp. 299–300.
26. For the famous metaphor which speaks of *man* as the "shepherd of Being," see Heidegger, *Holzwege*, p. 321.
27. See Walter A. Strauss, *Descent and Return: The Orphic Theme in Modern Literature* (Cambridge: Harvard University Press, 1971).
28. *The Complete Works of Horace*, ed. Casper J. Craemer, Jr. (New York: Modern Library, 1936), p. 410.

one whose calling is to assemble the *disjecta membra* of the earth and to build a world.[29]

The Orphic voice has, of course, been recurrently heard throughout the history of European literature, but Mr. Strauss is surely right in thinking it to belong in a special way to the modern period. For it was amidst the new conditions of life arising in the last years of the eighteenth century and the early decades of the following century that the poets most deeply responsive to the exigencies of the age began to have a sense of being irresistibly committed to a project of world-building.

The great shaping force in cultural life at the dawn of the nineteenth century was undoubtedly that iconoclastic spirit which was bequeathed the period by the whole scientific and critical effort of the Enlightenment. And the consequent reorientation of intelligence did for a time, it is true, bring a certain exhilaration, as the new horizons of science and thought induced the happy conviction that a great and wonderful gulf had been opened up between "now" and "then." "Bliss was it in that dawn to be alive,/But to be young," said Wordsworth ("French Revolution"), "was very heaven!"—or so at least to many it seemed, for a brief glorious moment, since everywhere the shackles of outmoded inheritances were being thrown off and since the new scene of life appeared increasingly to be under the sway of nothing more tyrannous than the unfettered and freely questing intelligence of man himself. Yet this bright prospect soon darkened, as the disheartening realization grew that now men bore, unaided and alone, the full "weight of all this unintelligible world." Blake was aghast at the "hard cold constrictive" climate into which the people of his age were moving and prayed (in his

29. It will be remembered that the Orpheus myth not only speaks of the singing poet's power to bring harmony and order to the earth but also apotheosizes his descent into Hades in quest of his beloved wife Eurydice and, finally, recounts its dirgeful tale of how he was subsequently torn apart by those female disciples of Dionysus known as the Maenads, his head thereafter floating down the river Hebros as it continued to sing and prophesy. These, says Walter Strauss, are the "three major 'moments' in . . . [the] myth" (*Descent and Return*, p. 6). But it is only the first of these "moments" that is being adumbrated in his essay—although, as Mr. Strauss reminds us, the concluding moment affirms quite as strongly as the first the indestructibility of that magic belonging to the Orphic power of song.

famous letter of 22 November 1802 to Thomas Butts) that they might be delivered "From single vision and Newton's sleep." There came a time when Wordsworth (in the "Immortality Ode") sadly remarked the fact that for him no longer were "meadow, grove, and stream,/The earth, and every common sight,/ . . . Apparelled in celestial light": "The things which I have seen I now can see no more." Nor could Keats resist the sense of angels' wings having been clipped, of "all charms" having been banished, of the very air having been emptied of "all mysteries"—by "cold philosophy" (*Lamia*). And similar testimonies were forthcoming from the French generation of Lamartine and from the German generation of Hölderlin and Novalis. The old sun that had lit up the universe for centuries was now eclipsed: the most basic categorical certainties that had perennially supported human life were all of a sudden at the point of withering away, under the "touch of cold philosophy"—and those who were most alert to the new situation felt themselves, therefore, to have been brought to bay at the farthermost extremities of the world.

But then, in addition to the metaphysical crisis, the years between 1789 and 1848 were also marked by social and political transmutations that profoundly affected the texture of Western life. The Revolution and the Napoleonic fanfarade brought immense excitements into the European community, and brought high expectations not only of the justice but also of the pomp and the glory that would be a part of the New Jerusalem. Yet, in point of fact, after the destruction of the *ancien régime* and the debacle of Waterloo there came nothing but the drab mediocrity of a bourgeois bureaucratism whose entrenchment throughout the remainder of the century guaranteed that long stasis sometimes blandly spoken of as "the hundred years' peace," which was, of course, not effectively disrupted until the outbreak of hostilities in 1914. And, furthermore, it was the fate of sensitive men to be required to reckon with the foundering of all radical hope while at the same time having to reckon with the new reality of the modern city, with its "dark Satanic mills" and its *anomie*, its crime and destitution, and its endlessly proliferating jumble of facelessness and disorder. "Hell," said Shelley in

1819 (in "Peter Bell the Third," pt. III), "is a city much like London—/A populous and a smoky city"; and he was by no means alone in his presentiment of something essentially infernal in the kinds of vast social collectivities newly brought into existence by the industrial revolution.

Now it was the conjunction of breakdown in the realm of fundamental faith with the emergence of social and political realities whose recalcitrancy seemed answerable to no large principle of meaning—it was this coincidence of religious and historical crisis that prepared an occasion for the poet's concluding that the imagination must be restored (in Stephen Spender's formulation) "to its position of Verb."[30]   Which is to say that, in the absence of order and value, the literary task came to be conceived as that of creating order and value, of creating indeed not an imitation or a mirror of the existing world but rather a "heterocosm"[31] or an alternative world that might offer the human spirit a more satisfactory ballast than any it could find in the world "out there."   Sometimes, of course, the kind of riposte which the literary imagination offered a broken world entailed not so much the creation of heterocosmic analogues as it did the angry and spiteful rejection of any kind of heterocosmic possibility, and it is this essentially antirational program of an Orphism soured and hopeless that one finds in the line that runs from Rimbaud and Lautréamont to the Surrealists, and on perhaps to contemporaries like Samuel Beckett and Maurice Blanchot.   But no doubt the more central impulse in modern literature has been the heterocosmic, and it is this radically Orphic strain—classically instanced by such figures as Novalis and Nerval, Mallarmé and Rilke—that Walter Strauss has brilliantly reviewed.

Mr. Strauss admits into his purview, however, neither the Anglo-American tradition in literature nor those writers who have plotted the major stratagems in the field of the novel.   And thus his account of the Orphic venture in the modern period is

30. Stephen Spender, *The Struggle of the Modern* (Berkeley and Los Angeles: University of California Press, 1963), p. 17.
31. The term is M. H. Abrams's: see his *The Mirror and the Lamp: Romantic Theory and the Critical Tradition* (New York: W. W. Norton & Co., The Norton Library, 1957), pp. 272–85.

one that is severely limited. When one looks, for example, at the English tradition, it will surely seem impossible to draw a fully adequate circle of definition about the Orphic pattern without taking into account the agenda of Blake and Wordsworth and Keats, and of Browning and Yeats. Quentin Anderson has recently argued with great forcefulness (in his book *The Imperial Self*)[32] that, in the American line, most of the great exemplars of the national imagination—from Whitman to Stevens—are wholly committed (in Henry James's phrase) to the "obstinate finality" of consciousness and to the intention, in the words of Emerson's Orphic poet, to "Build therefore your own world." Nor can one recall such monuments of modern fiction as *À la recherche du temps perdu* and *Finnegans Wake, Women in Love* and *Joseph und seine Brüder*, without being reminded that the great novelists of our period have, many of them, to quite as great a degree as our poets, been Magi—not necessarily in the sense of being engaged in any kind of occultist illuminism but in the sense of their dedication to the tasks of world-building and of restoring the imagination to its position of Verb. So the terrain over which Orpheus presides in the literature of the modern age is very large indeed.

Those who have patiently followed the long and intricately woven argument of Walter Strauss's *Descent and Return* will have noticed how definitely, at more than one point, he finds a bench mark for his subject in a word of Erich Heller to the effect that the prevalent tendency of that tradition of modern literature under the sign of Orpheus is one that moves toward a "progressive colonization of inwardness."[33] And so indeed it does. For when both nature and history begin no longer to be a glass of vision wherewith the hand of God is beheld and when, therefore, the created order begins to be experienced in terms primarily of its sheer givenness, and this very largely an affair of concealment

32. Quentin Anderson, *The Imperial Self* (New York: Vintage Books, 1972).
33. The theme is recurrent throughout Erich Heller's criticism: see, for example, his *The Hazard of Modern Poetry* (Cambridge: Bowes & Bowes, 1953), *passim*; or his "Rilke and Nietzsche," in *The Disinherited Mind* (Philadelphia: Dufour and Saifer, 1952), pp. 99–140; or his *The Artist's Journey into the Interior* (New York: Random House, 1965), chaps. III and V.

and enigma, then, inevitably, things will be felt to be haphazard, accidental—and, for this reason, gratuitous, extraneous, and only very minimally relevant to any effort at metaphysical reconstruction. Amidst such circumstances, it will be not unnatural for the literary imagination, believing itself to be surrounded by the *de trop*, to solicit what Geoffrey Hartman calls "the unmediated vision"[34] and to aim at encountering fundamental reality anew, in the nakedest possible way and without benefit of any intercessory agency. But since existence is everywhere overrun by the "Flood that rages without and drowns the meaning of things,"[35] the heirs of Orpheus will conclude, as they have generally done in the modern period, that the building of a world must necessarily involve an infinitizing of subjectivity, the "colonization of inwardness." Rilke—whom Mr. Strauss rightly regards as the purest modern example of the Orphic poet—says in the Seventh Duino Elegy, "Nirgends, Geliebte, wird Welt sein als innen" ("Nowhere, beloved, can world exist but within"). And it is a similar testimony that has been made, with varying degrees of radicalism, by the votaries of the Thracian *Meistersinger*, from Hölderlin to Eugenio Montale and from Coleridge to Yves Bonnefoy (to speak of poets at the beginning and end of the modern age whose idioms display immense diversity).

The tendency of the Orphic imagination to elect as its world a realm of Infinite Subjectivity must, however, call into question the appropriateness of its being regarded in certain areas of contemporary theology as exemplifying the kind of procedure whereby religious certainty may be renewed in our own late time. True, theological enterprise must undertake fundamental reconstruction, if it is once again powerfully to commend itself to the generality of educated men as a *possible* way of handling experience. And no doubt its best way of initiating this process of reconstruction will be one involving an attempt to apply (in Husserl's sense of the term) a certain *epochē* to much that comprises the formularies and protocols of its own funded tradition.

---

34. See Geoffrey H. Hartman, *The Unmediated Vision: An Interpretation of Wordsworth, Hopkins, Rilke and Valéry* (New Haven: Yale University Press, 1954).

35. Heller, *The Artist's Journey into the Interior*, p. 151.

For, only by "bracketing out" for a time many of its inherited systemizations, can it manage to take a step backward and thus pristinely recover (in a way that does not violate the established grammar of modern intelligence) something of that primal vision of the splendid munificence of Being which originally constituted man as the *homo religiosus*. In short, it must once again "step barefoot into reality"—and, again no doubt, it has much to learn from poetic discipline about how primary truth is to be "hailed" and spoken of.

So the Orphic way in poetry, in its intention to offer an "unmediated" world in which human sensibility may newly ground itself, will naturally seem at *our* juncture to furnish a highly significant *exemplum*. Yet its commitment, in the modern phase of poetry, to a radically individualist subjectivism must throw it somewhat into doubt. A venerated sage of this century did, to be sure, on one occasion venture the postulate that religion "is what the individual does with his own solitariness."[36] But it is a foolish proposition, for everything that man is and does and thinks has as its most essential setting the realm of what Martin Buber called "the interhuman."[37] It is no doubt, indeed, the writings of Buber that we think of most immediately today as having installed in contemporary consciousness a sense of the inherently transactional nature of human life, of the fact that we are men by virtue of being fellowmen, that our humanity is in its deepest essence an affair of "fellowmanhood."[38] But, preeminent as Buber has surely been in laying down this lesson, it has also (to say nothing of empirical social science) been steadily advanced in the modern period by a long and manifold tradition of *Lebensphilosophie* reaching, on the European scene, from Ludwig Feuerbach through Hermann Cohen and Franz Rosenzweig to Ferdinand Ebner and Eberhard Grisebach, to Eugen Rosenstock-Huessy and Karl Jaspers and Gabriel Marcel;

---

36. Alfred North Whitehead, *Religion in the Making* (New York: Macmillan Co., 1927), p. 16.
37. See Martin Buber, *The Knowledge of Man*, trans. Maurice Friedman and Ronald Gregor Smith (New York: Harper and Row, 1965), chap. III.
38. The phrase is the late Joseph Haroutunian's: see his *God with Us: A Theology of Transpersonal Life* (Philadelphia: Westminster Press, 1965), pp. 11–39.

and, of course, this line of thought often paralleled very closely the kind of philosophical anthropology developed by such American thinkers as George Herbert Mead and John Dewey. We inherit, in short, from the last hundred years an immense body of testimony which says in effect that human existence is radically and ineluctably "dialogic" in character, that selfhood is in fact literally constituted within the network of interpersonal relationship and is inconceivable except as an emergent from the world of I-and-Thou. As Buber says, "It is from one man to another that the heavenly bread of self-being is passed."[39] Nor does this emphasis represent any kind of distinctively modern discovery. On the contrary: it belongs to the most ancient wisdom of the race to know that "No man is an Iland, intire of it selfe . . . [but that] every man is a peece of the Continent . . . [and] a part of the maine. . . ."

Furthermore, it is just the fact of our being members one of another, of our being covenanted together by the nature of our common humanity—it is just this fact that has led the great modern specialists in *Religionswissenschaft* (Gerardus van der Leeuw, Joachim Wach, Raffaele Pettazzoni, Mircea Eliade) to see that the *sensus divinitatis* itself, in its most fundamental manifestations, is not a consequence of any explorations of the self-contained individual but, instead, arises primarily out of the rich fullness of man's dialogical experience. Which is to say that, since man, insofar as he remains truly human, can occupy no vantage point outside the dialogical world he shares with his brethren, the real center of gravity in the realm of his religious experience (as in every other realm of his life and thought bearing on fundamental questions of meaning and value) is to be located within that network of interpersonal exchange and commonalty which forms the matrix of his concrete existence. Religious affirmation makes reference, of course, to a dimension of reality transcending the dialogical world of human life. But Transcendence—at least in the traditions of Jewish and Christian faith—enunciates itself in and through those decisive moments in the life of a people when, by way of their dealings with one another, certain great paradigmatic images and archetypes

39. Buber, *The Knowledge of Man,* p. 71.

of reality emerge which, because they are felt to disclose the ultimate otherness with which men must reckon, gather the power of coordinating and directing human endeavor. And the encounter with ultimacy occurring not in some remote region of ideality but amidst the restless dynamism of the life of a people— on whose calendar the encounter-event may even sometimes be precisely datable—the memory of the redeeming *magnalia* must, therefore, be a primary agency of the religious imagination, since it finds the history of the *Volk*, at once in the terms of judgment and of grace, to be in part the medium of the great decisive disclosures and revelations.

So, in a period of religious reconstruction such as our own, it would seem that, however much the *via poetica* in its Orphic mode may be felt to afford a guiding model, our search ought surely to be for large examples of the poetic imagination proceeding to build—or to rebuild—our human world with reference to its essentially dialogic and historical character. And it is just as we begin from this standpoint to sift and probe our modern inheritance in literature that we may win a freshened sense of how urgent is the pressure that T. S. Eliot's legacy continues to exert upon us. For when one thinks of Mallarmé's commitment to a *poésie pure*, of Rilke's dedication to his terrible Angels, of Valéry's vision of poetry as a "closed palace of mirrors," of Yeats's lust for various apocalyptic extremities, of Pound's "moral nihilism charged with moral fury,"[40] of Stevens's conviction that "Reality is a cliché from which we escape by metaphor"[41]—when one thinks of the characteristic attitudes and stratagems belonging to the great classic canon of modern poetry, it must surely be felt to be Eliot, more so perhaps than most of the other great figures of the age, who presents us with a "poetry of simple civic virtue,"[42] a poetry, that is, whose world is not the *Weltinnenraum* (world space interiorized) of the Orphic imagination but the dialogic and historical reality of the human City itself.

40. The phrase is Michael Polanyi's: see his "On the Modern Mind," in *Encounter*, vol. 24, no. 5 (May 1965), p. 19.
41. Wallace Stevens, "Adagia," in *Opus Posthumous* (New York: Alfred A. Knopf, 1957), p. 179.
42. Heller, *The Hazard of Modern Poetry*, p. 38.

His exemplary role in this regard is, of course, one conferred upon him by the cycle of poems that makes the crowning achievement of his career, the sequence which began with "Burnt Norton" of 1935 and which concluded with the appearance of "Little Gidding" in the autumn of 1942. The imagination controlling "Prufrock" and "Gerontion," *The Waste Land* and "The Hollow Men" was, to be sure, one that had never been infatuated with the Orphic vision of the poet as *vates sacer*, and thus its basic allegiance had never been to any heterocosmic reality of its own. On the contrary: the poet of "Gerontion" and *The Waste Land* was one primarily interested in setting forth the human world under the aspect of its ineradicable historicity. Which is to say that his way of plotting experience reflected a view of men's lives as thoroughly embedded in temporal process and as inextricably entangled with one another, so much so indeed as to rule out of court the possibility of any absolute beginnings, each individual being the result of all the irrevocable commitments and actions previously undertaken at once by himself and those others to whom his life has been related. Gerontion is "an old man in a dry month" who dwells in a decayed and draughty house, and in a world of "cunning passages, contrived corridors," a world haunted by the ghosts of those who deceived "with whispering ambitions" and who were guided by nothing but vanity. And Tiresias, that spectral witness of the broken world scanned by *The Waste Land*, marvels at the various evidences that "death had undone so many": nor can the shards and fragments shored up against the ruins of European civilization arrest the slumping drift of

> Falling towers
> Jerusalem Athens Alexandria
> Vienna London
> Unreal

Indeed, the predominant impression conveyed by Eliot's poetry from the time of *Prufrock and Other Observations* (1917) to that of "The Hollow Men" (1925) is an impression of stoppage and closure. Gerontion knows that in "the juvescence of the year/Came Christ the tiger," but, also knowing himself to dwell in a "Depraved May," he wonders "what forgiveness" there may be "After such knowledge"—just as the Pilgrim in *The Waste Land*, having given no proper reply to those imperative syllables uttered by the divine voice ("Da Da Da"—"give, sympathize, control"), knows himself to be irredeemably consigned to the arid plain stretching before him. The world has grown old, and its amassment of failure and malfeasance, of blunder and botched opportunity, imposes now a weight of burdens too overwhelming to permit any fresh start: it is such a view of the human prospect that informed the first major phase of Eliot's testimony.

In the period extending from the late 1920s into the early years of the following decade, as he was ever more deeply exploring what was implied by the Christian position he had lately embraced, Eliot began, however, to be persuaded that, disabling though the burdens imposed by our human heritage may be, our most essential task remains that of seeking to "fare forward." Since there is no other dwelling-place for us but historical time, he began to conclude that, despite all the taint and ambiguity in our history, there can be no escaping the truth that "Only through time time is conquered" ("Burnt Norton") and that "the way forward is the way back" ("The Dry Salvages"). For, as he felt, though there may be "only a limited value/In the knowledge derived from experience" ("East Coker"), no new access to hope and health can be found apart from a deep appropriation of the roots from which we are sprung, apart from a deep repossession of that complex manifold of ordeal and humiliation and glory which constitutes the soil in actual experience out of which the human City has come.

It is in fact the commitment to anamnesis as the way of rebuilding a world for the imagination that establishes the quaternal character of the poems that Eliot brought together in 1943 under the title *Four Quartets*. Nearly every critic of the past twenty-five years who has advanced any sort of sustained argument about the cycle has felt obliged to fashion some elaborate proposal about the meaning of the musical analogy implicit in Eliot's title; and these postulations have generally tended to soar off on flights so highly speculative as to leave behind, unillumined, the textual actuality of the poems themselves. But surely the Swedish critic Staffan Bergsten is, of all these scholiasts, the

most helpful, in his simple and immediately persuasive suggestion that it is "Burnt Norton" which gives the clue as to the
nature of the quaternity belonging to each of the four poems.
The poem of 1935 begins by saying that

> Time present and time past
> Are both perhaps present in time future . . . .

Then, in its IInd movement, "Burnt Norton" relates time present,
time past, and time future to that "still point of the turning
world"—"Where past and future are gathered"—which is nothing other than eternity. Accordingly, since it is the interrelation-
ship between these four dimensions that is being constantly
orchestrated in each of the four poems, Mr. Bergsten very sensi-
bly suggests that each poem in the four-part sequence may,
indeed, be considered a "quartet," for in each four "dimensions"
(the past, the present, the future, and eternity) are being "in-
terrelated as the voices or instruments in a musical quartet."[43]

And so indeed it is throughout the entire sequence, from the
beginning of "Burnt Norton" to the conclusion of "Little Gidding": what is everywhere being meditated upon is the inelucta-
ble historicity of our life-world. Which is to say that the poems
are contemplating the fact that man is so made and so situated
that he can never win through to fulfillment by way merely of
appropriating the present moment, since he is by his nature
invested with responsibility at once for the heritage of the past
and for the shape of the future. He is always *homo viator,* one
entrained towards what is yet to come. But he is never simply at
the mercy of historical process: through reason and memory and
imagination he can transcend the causalities of nature and history, and thus there is no moment of his life which may not
become eschatological—with new meanings breaking in, with
new beginnings becoming possible. So, for all its embeddedness
in time past and time present and time future, human life is also
open to the ingression of "eternity"; and it is just its situation at a
point of juncture between the temporal and the eternal which
makes for the special kind of complexity being rendered by the

43. Staffan Bergsten, *Time and Eternity: A Study in the Structure and
Symbolism of T. S. Eliot's Four Quartets* (Bonniers-Stockholm: Svenska
Bokförlaget, 1960), p. 140.

four "voices" that are contrapuntally harmonized in each of the *Quartets*.

But, though Eliot was never in the early years of his career basically committed to an Orphic sense of the poet's mission (as that of one building a world *ab ovo*), once he emphatically elected a Christian perspective, he did for a time become a sort of "new" Orpheus. For, knowing himself now to be *against* the prevalent dispositions of a secular climate and feeling obliged to rescue the Christian archetypes from their hackneyed vapidity, a major part of his endeavor inevitably came to be that of making such detours as would enable him at all costs to avoid the associations of what the Anglican religious, Brother George Every, has somewhere called "Christmas-card Gothic." So the impression conveyed, for example, by "Ash Wednesday" is very much that of a man building up almost anew, out of his own inventiveness, the whole world of the Christian mythos: indeed, at a certain crucial point, the poem's protagonist says:

> Because I cannot hope to turn again
> Consequently I rejoice, having to construct something
> Upon which to rejoice. . . .

And, despite the large use being made of the Church's liturgical idiom, the air of the entire poem is that of an intensely subjectivistic and essentially private mythology.[44]

It is quite a different atmosphere, however, that we meet in the *Quartets*. For, by the time Eliot had entered that phase of his career which was to be crowned by this supreme accomplishment, he had grown sufficiently nonchalant about his religious commitment to be able to remember again the lesson he had taught himself many years earlier, that the progress of a poet needs to be "continual self-sacrifice, a continual extinction of personality," that his highest obligation is not to dwell in some newly begotten universe of his own but is rather to "surrender . . . himself . . . to something which is more valuable."[45] And, in

44. This view of "Ash Wednesday" has been argued at length and with great cogency by Vincent Buckley: see his *Poetry and the Sacred* (London: Chatto & Windus, 1968), pp. 214–19.
45. T. S. Eliot, "Tradition and the Individual Talent," in *Selected Essays: 1917–1932* (New York: Harcourt, Brace and Co., 1947), pp. 6–7.

the years of his full maturity, that to which he had come to want most deeply to surrender himself was "the pattern" which is made by the world of the human City, in its perdurance through the seasons and cycles of historical time. Thus we ought not to find it surprising that the poetry of the *Quartets* is a poetry vibrant not with

> . . . the experience of one life only
> But of many generations. . . .

Which is, of course, why (as "The Dry Salvages" reminds us) the whole logic of the enterprise requires

> The backward look behind the assurance
> Of recorded history, the backward half-look
> Over the shoulder, towards the primitive terror.

Like many great works of art, the whole sequence making up the *Quartets* happened in part by way of accident. "Burnt Norton" was put together out of fragments eliminated from an early draft of Eliot's play of 1935, *Murder in the Cathedral*, and it was conceived as a single poem. Then, as he remarked many years later in an interview he granted John Lehmann (published in *The New York Times Book Review*, 29 November 1953), "East Coker" was begun quite by chance, after the outbreak of World War II; and, as he said, it was only as the design of this work gradually came to light that he began at last to foresee a cycle of four long poems. "East Coker" was published in the *New English Weekly* in March of 1940, and, in quick succession, it was followed by "The Dry Salvages" in 1941 and by "Little Gidding" in 1942. Yet the cycle, however adventitiously it came into existence, discloses, when viewed as a whole, a very remarkable concentration of purpose and unity of emphasis. For, everywhere, it records a single search—for the ultimate pattern of meaning that may be descried amidst the invincible historicity of the human condition. We are creatures who "live from that which is no more toward what is not yet through a slender, fragile boundary called 'now.' "[46] And not only are the limiting circumstances of one's life essentially temporal, but so

46. Roger Hazelton, *God's Way with Man: Variations on the Theme of Providence* (New York-Nashville: Abingdon Press, 1956), p. 101.

too also are all the codes and beliefs and institutions that give form and substance to one's life: they *"present* themselves to me . . . as a precipitate of what has happened, of what they have been in the lives of earlier men, whose enforced heir I am."[47] Which is to say that the essence of the human reality is historical and that we belong to what "Little Gidding" calls "time's convenant." But is man's life, then, just "the trailing/Consequence of further days and hours" and a matter of "mere sequence"? "History may be servitude,/History may be freedom," says "Little Gidding," but in relation to what kind of orientation or perspective does it become the one or the other? It is this kind of question which is constantly at the center of the meditation being carried on in the *Four Quartets.*

The English critic Bernard Bergonzi remarks in his recent book on Eliot that, though Dunkirk and the fall of France and the Battle of Britain loomed over the years in which most of the cycle was produced, "one sees little sign of these events in Eliot's writing."[48] And it is an astonishing judgment, for the poems are in point of fact drenched in the calamitous realities of their period, none indeed so much as the poem of 1940, "East Coker," which, more suggestively perhaps than any of the others, may put us in mind of the central drift of the entire sequence.

In the little book called *The Idea of a Christian Society,* which appeared in 1939, as he looked back upon the sad month of the previous year in which Édouard Daladier and Neville Chamberlain had sealed at Munich the Anglo-French accords with Hitler that signalized the collapse of Europe, Eliot said:

> I believe that there must be many persons who, like myself, were deeply shaken by the events of September 1938, in a way from which one does not recover; persons to whom that month brought a profounder realisation of a general plight. . . . The feeling which was new and unexpected was a feeling of humiliation, which seemed to demand an act of personal contrition, of humility, repentance and amendment; what had happened was something in which one was deeply implicated and responsible. It was . . . a doubt of the validity of a civilisation. . . .

47. Julián Marías, *Reason and Life,* trans. Kenneth S. Reid and Edward Sarmiento (New Haven: Yale University Press, 1956), pp. 113–14.
48. Bernard Bergonzi, *T. S. Eliot* (New York: Collier Books, 1972), p. 151.

Was our society, which had always been so assured of its supe-
riority and rectitude, so confident of its unexamined premisses,
assembled round anything more permanent than a congeries of
banks, insurance companies and industries, and had it any beliefs more essential than a belief in compound interest and the
maintenance of dividends?[49]

And, in these sentiments, Eliot was sharing the widespread and
profound unease that the Munich Pact called forth, in its apparent foretokening of general disintegration.

One imagines, then, that in the months that immediately followed, as the West seemed everywhere veering toward utter
capitulation to the barbarities of Nazism, he began to be deeply
struck by the large irony presented by a civilization whose last
state was so much worse than the first. For in that morning-time
of the Renaissance, when the basic terms of the modern West
were being set, men had counted on the future to bring a
redemption of the human community from all the disorders and
iniquities of the Dark Ages: the world had been thought to be
at last on an escalator that would henceforth carry it ever on-
ward and upward, toward that happy condition which an
Englishman of the sixteenth century named Utopia. But, alas,
in the winter of 1939, far from anything like Sir Thomas More's
dream having been realized, it was the demonic atavism of the
Third Reich that appeared to be the wave of the future. The
high optimism surrounding the birth of the modern world had
finally given way to, may even have prepared the way for, the
new terrors that were sweeping across the European scene. The
children of light, possibly because of the foolish illusions they
had indulged, were by way of being undone by the children of
darkness, and it was a time in which men were bound to be
overborne by a sense of the strange ways in which the course of
history outruns the range of human intention.

So it was not unnatural that Eliot should have been led to
recall his own remote ancestor, Sir Thomas Elyot, whose birth-
place (in the little village of Coker in Somersetshire) he had
visited in the summer of 1937. For this Tudor humanist—loyal
adjutant to Henry the Eighth and friend to Sir Thomas More—

49. T. S. Eliot, *The Idea of a Christian Society* (London: Faber and
Faber, 1939), pp. 63–64.

despite his fidelity to the churchmanship of Cranmer, had been one thoroughly committed to the kind of high confidence about the historical destiny of man that he had learnt from such luminaries as Pico della Mirandola and Erasmus and that informed his own various writings (most notably, his treatise of 1531, *The Boke named The Gouvernour*). Indeed, he, as it seemed, could be thought of as one of those "quiet-voiced elders" of that earlier time who had bequeathed "merely a receipt for deceit" to the world that at the end of the 1930s was about to be engulfed in the second general war of a century still young. And thus it occurred to the poet of "East Coker" to reflect: "In my beginning is my end."

This phrase, "In my beginning is my end," as it makes a kind of leitmotiv throughout the music of "East Coker," does in fact establish a major theme of the poem which wants to speak about how "Houses"—by which is meant not only families but also nations and institutions and ways of thought—about how

> Houses rise and fall, crumble, are extended
> Are removed, destroyed, restored. . . .
> Old stone to new building, old timber to new fires,
> Old fires to ashes, and ashes to the earth. . . .
> Houses live and die. . . .

What is being called to mind is that fearsome law whereby, in the language of Isaac Watts's old hymn, "Time, like an ever-rolling stream,/Bears all its sons away." So, however much merriment and dancing at night there may have been long ago on the greens of the Somersetshire village out of which Thomas Elyot came ("Two and two, necessarye coniunction,/Holding eche other by the hand or the arm"), the rhythms that were kept by those goodly people are now to be seen as having all been an affair of the larger cadence of *corso* and *ricorso*—of "Feet rising and falling/Eating and drinking. Dung and death." And the poem asks, therefore, what profit there can possibly be in our own late time in turning back to that distant dawn of the modern world:

> What is the late November doing
> With the disturbance of the spring
> And creatures of the summer heat . . . ?

For we are

> In the middle, not only in the middle of the way
> But all the way, in a dark wood, in a bramble,
> On the edge of a grimpen, where is no secure foothold,
> And menaced by monsters. . . .

Indeed, our being now lostlings in a dark wood may be a result of the generation of Sir Thomas Elyot having "deceived us/Or deceived themselves," of their having bequeathed us a kind of penchant for utopian illusions that has rendered us incompetent to reckon soberly with the hazards of history. So, says Eliot,

> Do not let me hear
> Of the wisdom of old men, but rather of their folly,
> Their fear of fear and frenzy, their fear of possession,
> Of belonging to another, or to others, or to God.

Yet, as this poet looked out upon the dilapidation of the world-scene of his own period, he found it impossible to regard those faraway people of the English Renaissance as having been markedly less wise than his own generation ("The only wisdom we can hope to acquire/Is the wisdom of humility"). For, on the eve of World War II, there were none who could offer a compass to steer by, and everything seemed to be disintegrating:

> They all go into the dark . . .
> The captains, merchant bankers, eminent men of letters,
> The generous patrons of art, the statesmen and the rulers,
> Distinguished civil servants, chairmen of many committees,
> Industrial lords and petty contractors, all go into the dark,
> And dark the Sun and Moon, and the Almanach de Gotha
> And the Stock Exchange Gazette, the Directory of Directors,
> And cold the sense and lost the motive of action.

The logic at work in "East Coker" intends, however, to suggest that it may be precisely in such a twilight hour of impotence and confusion of spirit, when all specious securities have been destroyed, that men can begin truly to discern the full actuality of their plight. And it is assumed that real "acceptation of the cross of conditions"[50] is imperative, since the patient may not

50. Nicodemus, *Renascence: An Essay in Faith* (London: Faber and Faber, 1943), p. 55. ("Nicodemus" was the pseudonym occasionally employed by the late Melville Chaning-Pearce.)

be cured unless he acknowledges that he is ill. Thus no sooner does the poem contemplate how total is the darkness settling down upon the Western world in 1939 than it begins to invoke the *via negativa* of St. John of the Cross: "be still, and let the dark come upon you"—

> You must go by a way wherein there is no ecstasy.
> In order to arrive at what you do not know
> You must go by a way which is the way of ignorance.
> In order to possess what you do not possess
> You must go by the way of dispossession.
> In order to arrive at what you are not
> You must go through the way in which you are not.
> And what you do not know is the only thing you know. . . .

Eliot's recommendation of the Negative Way, of the way of descent into darkness and deprivation, is, of course, frequently declared to express a kind of Gnostic intention to obliterate, or to find a means of seceding from, the exigent realities of historical time. But in truth it is, on the contrary, a stratagem bidding for careful and sober confrontation of those realities. And what is being assumed is that we shall find a route into hope and health never by evading but only by facing into the crises and distempers of history. For, as Keats says (in *Hyperion*),

> . . . to bear all naked truths,
> And to envisage circumstance, all calm,
> That is the top of sovereignty.

True, we like to think that we are "sound, substantial flesh and blood," but ours in fact is a world endowed by Adam, "the ruined millionaire," and thus whatever we achieve of worth and value must be consequent upon our managing to become twice-born men. As Reinhold Niebuhr once remarked, "All birth in the realm of man's historic institutions is rebirth. The old self must die in order that the new self may be born. . . . But the new self, whether in men or in nations, can not be born if the old self evades the death of repentance, seeking rather to establish itself in its old security and old isolation."[51] So Eliot says, ". . . let the dark come upon you," for then in due season "the

51. Reinhold Niebuhr, *Discerning the Signs of the Times* (New York: Charles Scribner's Sons, 1946), p. 45.

darkness shall be the light, and the stillness the dancing." The dialectic being proposed, in other words, is the procedure anciently defined in St. Augustine's formula, *descendite ut ascendatis.*

But the descent into darkness, as "East Coker" reminds us, will involve not merely a repossession of

> . . . the lifetime of one man only
> But of old stones that cannot be deciphered.
> There is a time for the evening under starlight,
> A time for the evening under lamplight
> (The evening with the photograph album).

The "old stones that cannot be deciphered" are, presumably, the tombstones of the Coker churchyard, and they stand for that which is being spoken of in the opening sentence of the final strophe—"Home is where one starts from." That is to say, the true pattern of life is to be found not in "the experience of one life only/But [in that] of many generations" ("The Dry Salvages"), and thus the recovery of that pattern must entail a journey backward, in part for the sake of winning insight into how error was bred in the bone. We are sprung from the dead, and (as "Little Gidding" says)

> . . . what the dead had no speech for, when living,
> They can tell you, being dead: the communication
> Of the dead is tongued with fire beyond the language of the living.

It is good, then, at "evening under lamplight," to peer at the pages of family albums, for we need to be explorers. "And the end of all our exploring/Will be to arrive where we started/And know the place for the first time" ("Little Gidding"). So, dark as the human prospect seemed at the time of Dunkirk and discouraging as in many ways the inheritance from the past appeared to be, having been reminded by the journey backward to his own roots in the village of Coker that the way leading upward is one that must first go downward, Eliot's way of concluding "East Coker" is by no means dispirited: "We must be still and still moving/Into another intensity/For a further union, a deeper communion. . . ."

Now it is such a structure of thought that makes the basis of

Eliot's design throughout the culminating poetry of his career. In a sentence whose rhetorical piquancy proffers a counterfeit punctiliousness, the late Philip Rahv charged that Eliot was always "conducting a campaign against history precisely in the name of history."[52] But nothing could be further from the truth, at least in regard to the poet of the *Quartets,* for his abiding axiom is that only through and by means of what man is given in historical time can he make his way to felicity and blessedness, when "all shall be well and/All manner of thing shall be well." Eliot does not, of course, conceive the historicity of human existence to belong wholly to the dimension of the ordinary and the quotidian, to that before-and-afterness which constitutes the dimension of *chronos.* For the hours and days measured by clocks and calendars are ever and again interfused with moments of granted clarity that somehow bestow intelligibility and significance on the apparent haphazardness of all other moments. Then it is that we have a sense of having been rescued from the various ruts and entanglements that have held us captive to confusion and purposelessness, and all the scattered fragments of our lives are brought, as it were, to a point of convergence—or rearrange themselves in relation to some new pattern of meaning that brings joy and gladness to the heart. This, as Eliot says (in "Choruses from 'The Rock'"), is

> A moment not out of time, but in time, in what
> we call history: transecting, bisecting the
> world of time, a moment in time but not
> like a moment of time,
> A moment in time but time was made through
> that moment: for without the meaning there
> is no time, and that moment of time gave
> the meaning.

And when we are here—"At the still point of the turning world" —we dwell not in the time that is ticked off by chronometers but in the *right* time, the *fulfilled* time, the dimension of *kairos.*

Eliot does, indeed, situate the actual scene of human life amidst the traffic moving back and forth between the two worlds

52. Philip Rahv, *Literature and the Sixth Sense* (Boston: Houghton Mifflin Co., 1969), p. 211.

of *chronos* and *kairos*. It is a kind of crossroads, where time and eternity meet: or rather, in his conception, our human world of time present and time past and time future is recurrently transected and bisected by moments of disclosure and discernment that come all of a sudden—as "Burnt Norton" says, like "a shaft of sunlight." And Eliot's commitment to the Christian faith leads him to think of these moments as echoes of the Incarnation. But his preoccupation with the decisive situations of disclosure that punctuate our pilgrimage—with those moments of our experience (as the symbology of the *Quartets* puts it) in the Garden—does not usually entail any sort of individualistic mysticism. For, as he says in "Choruses from 'The Rock,'"

> What life have you if you have not life together?
> There is no life that is not in community. . . .

We are members one of another, and our deepest wisdom will be found to be a matter "of many generations." So, again and again throughout the *Quartets*, the protagonist of the poems finds his own destiny inwrought knottily into the larger destiny of humankind which is like "music heard so deeply/That it is not heard at all." It is, therefore, the historical imagination wherewith (in Henry James's phrase) "the figure in the carpet" is descried, and the pattern of man's passage through time is conceived to be the very language of God himself.

For all his reliance on memory and the historical imagination as the primary instruments of "foundational" thinking, Eliot never wants, however, to roam through the legacies of history in the spirit merely of a tourist or of an empirical researcher. In, for example, the last of the *Quartets* he recalls a visit he once made to the manor of Little Gidding, where, in the Huntingdonshire countryside, the distinguished Cambridge scholar Nicholas Ferrar established an Anglican religious community in 1625. It was a foundation with which two of the most distinguished poets of the age, Richard Crashaw and George Herbert, had attachments, and, on three occasions, it received as a visitor no less a personage than Charles the First, whose last sojourn there followed his vanquishment at Naseby in 1645. After the house was seized and plundered, however, by Cromwell's troops in

November of 1646, it was never rebuilt, though its chapel was renovated in 1714 and still stands as one of the English Church's great old monuments of Catholic piety. And it is his pilgrimage one winter afternoon to this hallowed memorial that Eliot is recalling in the poem which bears as its title the name of Ferrar's community. "Taking the route you would be likely to take/From the place you would be likely to come from," he makes his way along a country road to the chapel at Little Gidding. "And what you thought you came for," he says,

> Is only a shell, a husk of meaning
> From which the purpose breaks only when it is fulfilled
> If at all. Either you had no purpose
> Or the purpose is beyond the end you figured
> And is altered in fulfilment.

By which he means that to approach this blessed place as merely a casual tourist, as one having only a certain moderate curiosity about a national landmark, is to find at Little Gidding nothing more than "a shell, a husk of meaning":

> If you came this way,
> Taking any route, starting from anywhere,
> At any time or at any season,
> It would always be the same: you would have to put off
> Sense and notion. You are not here to verify,
> Instruct yourself, or inform curiosity
> Or carry report. You are here to kneel
> Where prayer has been valid.

This holy place, steeped as it is in the experience of a people, may, in other words, become a "figure" of man's ultimate fulfillment, if it is beheld not simply as a tourist's bourn but as at least having been for some "the world's end." One must "put off/Sense and notion": one must set aside the surmises and hypotheses, however ingenious, of mere opinion, for one comes not "to verify" some minor detail of the cloistered life in the English seventeenth century but rather to seek a truly vital relationship with the people whose prayer was validated in these sacred precincts. Indeed, to recall what is being spoken of in the Church's declarations about the "communion of saints" is to know that the archival and locational details of the life shared in by Ferrar's brethren are so little of the essence of what they had together that this place may even be said to be at once "England and nowhere. Never and always."

So it is that Eliot invites us to enter the *mysterion* of history, as he himself regularly sought to approach the passages and corridors through which the human pilgrimage has moved—with a great eagerness for empathy (since one's own identity is to be found only by way of a heremeneutic of the historical) and with such a humility as may facilitate the flow of messages from those who, being dead, are "tongued with fire beyond the language of the living." As he says in "Little Gidding,"

> This is the use of memory:
> For liberation—not less of love but expanding
> Of love beyond desire, and so liberation
> From the future as well as the past. . . .
> . . . History may be servitude,
> History may be freedom, See, now they vanish,
> The faces and places, with the self which, as it could, loved them,
> To become renewed, transfigured, in another pattern.

And throughout all his meditations on the way we are in history as fish are in water, on the infrangibility of our commitment to the *Polis*, to the life of the human City—throughout all this there runs, as a minor but recurrent melody, a further meditation on the office of the poet. But, on this level of things, far from embracing any Orphic vision of the poetic vocation, he wants rather to say (as in the great line in "East Coker") that "The poetry does not matter." True, the poet's labor is always something arduous and fraught with frustration: it entails an "intolerable wrestle/With words" which "strain,/Crack and sometimes break, under the burden,/Under the tension"—and

> . . . each venture
> Is a new beginning, a raid on the inarticulate
> With shabby equipment always deteriorating
> In the general mess of imprecision of feeling,
> Undisciplined squads of emotion. And what there is to conquer
> By strength and submission, has already been discovered
> Once or twice, or several times, by men whom one cannot hope
> To emulate—but there is no competition—
> There is only the fight to recover what has been lost

And found and lost again and again: and now, under conditions
That seem unpropitious.   But perhaps neither gain nor loss.
For us, there is only the trying.   The rest is not our business.

Yet, despite the strenuous exertions that are exacted by the poet's special kind of endeavor, it is not the poetry that matters, not some unexampled world that is brought into existence *ex nihilo* by the poetic word.   For, in Eliot's view of the matter, the dedicated poet purposes only

> To purify the dialect of the tribe
> And urge the mind to aftersight and foresight. . . .

He conceives the poet's task, in other words, to involve nothing more exalted than an effort at so putting in order our speech as to make the human word an instrument clean and supple enough to be a fit vehicle for the upbuilding of the City, for love of neighbor and praise of God—"The complete consort dancing together."   And one feels, indeed, that, whatever may be its dubieties and imperfections, the poetry of this modest, diffident genius is, as Erich Heller says, a "poetry of simple civic virtue."

Moreover, in a period when the religious imagination is seeking newly to ground itself in "foundational" thinking and is in effect being invited to find its model for this kind of endeavor in the Orphic modes of poetic art, it is precisely the deep involvement of Eliot's poetry in civic ethos that enables it to present an alternative model of foundational reflection, and one that may perhaps finally prove to be more salutary.

The effort to think religiously about experience is not, of course, an undertaking that requires some special talent or taste and which may, therefore, simply be let alone, if one considers oneself to be unendowed with the requisite propensity.   Nor is it an endeavor appropriate only to those who are members of a special sect or guild, such as churchmen or seminarians or professional theologians.   On the contrary: the act of religious reflection is the act that all men are performing at whatever point they begin to search their experience, at the level of *theos* or of ultimate meaning, for the guaranty or sanction that finally gives warrant to human existence.   Yet, in speaking of what authentic religious inquiry intends, to use a language (of "warrant" and "guaranty") whose flavor is moderately forensic is already somewhat to have falsified the case, since what is at issue is not matters of formal assurance but the question as to the possibility of a kind of Pascalian wager, that the world of our habitancy is so constituted as to be, in its basic tendency, supportive rather than spendthrift of the human enterprise. It is, indeed, the felt need for assurance of the possibility of such a wager being made that is deeply a part of the hopes and expectancies that men bring to the world, even when their cultural environment is one representing radical secularization.

The German Lutheran pastor Horst Symanowski, whose ministry in industrial areas since the close of the Second World War has been a remarkably prophetic influence on the European scene in recent years, reminds us, however, that in our period the form of the distinctively religious question will not generally be what it was in the world of the sixteenth century, when, as Luther expressed it, it was the question that said: "How can I find a gracious God?" This, it is true, was once the great question, and Luther's great way of answering it—"By faith alone!" —did over a long stretch of time satisfy the kind of imagination that issued from the wellsprings of the Protestant Reformation. But now, at the end of the modern age, the word *God* is a dead word that has very largely lost its power to focalize or to name Transcendence. Which does not at all mean, however, that the essential nerve of religious experience has been broken, for ever and again men continue to be brought "up against that which is not pliable and disposable, [against] . . . those hard edges [of the world] where . . . [they] are both stopped and challenged to move ahead"[53]—though, today, the truly crucial experiences of the Wholly Other are likely most often to be mediated by way of the *Polis*, by way of that network of human relationship that constitutes the environing scene of the individual's career. And thus in our own time the hunger for religious certainty, for the assurance that the otherness by which we are surrounded is *for* us rather than *against* us, finds its most characteristic expression, as Pastor Symanowski contends, in the question that says:

53. Harvey Cox, *The Secular City* (New York: Macmillan Co., 1965), p. 262.

" 'How can I find a gracious neighbor?' "[54]   It is not, of course, that the word *God* has somehow become translatable, exhaustively and without remainder, into the word *neighbor.*   Nor is it the case that the encounter with Transcendence is no longer a significant feature of human experience.   The new fact is rather that, no longer conceiving themselves to dwell at a point of intersection between Nature and Supernature, the people of our age, since it is the interpersonal world of the human community itself to which they find themselves most deeply committed, do therefore experience "the dimension of ultimacy"[55] in and through the claim that is laid upon them by the lives of those others bordering on their own.

The distinguished Scots theologian, the late Ronald Gregor Smith, suggested in one of his essays that the religious imagination is most fundamentally concerned with what men "do not and never can possess at all, as part of their self-equipment or as material for their self-mastery."[56]   And it is this *limit*—which *is* Transcendence—that we face, when we are *addressed* by a stranger or a neighbor.   For then we realize that we are, indeed, "confronting another agent who is himself an independent center of consciousness, who has his own perspectives, his own purposes, and his own desires to explore and to subdue the . . . world."[57]   Whereupon immediately the great issue arises as to whether we can somehow manage to live together in peace, each finding his bounden duty and succor in "the sacrament of the brother."[58]

So when Lionel Trilling tells us that "our fate, for better or worse, is political,"[59] he is simply summarizing a central theme

54. Horst Symanowski, *The Christian Witness in an Industrial Society,* trans. George H. Kehm (Philadelphia: Westminster Press, 1964), p. 50.

55. Langdon Gilkey, *Naming the Whirlwind: The Renewal of God-Language* (Indianapolis–New York: Bobbs-Merrill Co., 1969), p. 306.

56. Ronald Gregor Smith, *The Whole Man: Studies in Christian Anthropology* (Philadelphia: Westminster Press, 1969), p. 29.

57. Nathan A. Scott, Jr., *The Unquiet Vision: Mirrors of Man in Existentialism* (New York–Cleveland: World Publishing Co., 1969), p. 167.

58. Hans Urs von Balthasar, *Science, Religion and Christianity,* trans. Hilda Graef (Westminster, Md.: Newman Press, 1958), p. 142.

59. Lionel Trilling, *The Liberal Imagination* (New York: Viking Press, 1950), p. 100.

of modern consciousness, that the locus of the most urgent meanings of our lives is precisely that web of interpersonal reciprocity which makes up the life of the *Polis*, of the human City. For here it is—in the realm, as Buber calls it, of "the interhuman," where the light of our being is "a dialogical light"[60]—that we meet the realities in terms of which we must reckon with what is ultimately Deep in "the burthen of the mystery."

Undoubtedly, it is necessary today for the strategists of religious thought—and they include many others, of course, in contemporary cultural life beside academic theologians—to take what the *avant-garde* in German theology calls *ein Schritt zurück* (a step backward), behind the timeworn formularies of theological tradition, in order that the essentials of "foundational" thinking may be got straight. And it is a by no means unhappy development that those who are reflecting most deeply on the religious crisis of our period should today often be prepared to think of the poetic enterprise as having a significant tuitionary role in relation to their whole endeavor. For it is indeed a part of the poet's office to coin a language for experience so immaculate as in effect to convey to us, by the very purity of its candor, something like Stevens's word—

> Throw away the lights, the definitions,
> And say of what you see in the dark
> That it is this or that it is that,
> But do not use the rotted names.[61]

Yet, given the inherently dialogic and historical character of our actual world, we shall find no good model for its repossession in the world-building of those who follow in the train of Orpheus unless they, in the manner of the poet of *Four Quartets*, propose a world in which the primal human reality is an affair "of many generations" and of faring forward in the terms of I-and-thou.

Nor should it go unremarked that Martin Heidegger, who is in great measure responsible for the status presently accorded poetry as a prototype of "foundational" thought and who would seem prepared to offer large endorsement to the poetic imagina-

60. Urs von Balthasar, *Science, Religion and Christianity*, p. 49.
61. Stevens, 'The Man with the Blue Guitar," in *Collected Poems*, p. 183.

tion in its Orphic mode, does himself appear finally to be disinclined to release the literary enterprise from its commitment to the basic communal realities of human life. In, for example, his essay on "Hölderlin and the Essence of Poetry," he is meditating on a fragment from a draft of an unfinished poem of Hölderlin's—

> Much has man learnt.
> Many of the heavenly ones has he named,
> Since we have been a conversation
> And have been able to hear from one another.

And, as he picks his way through this brief passage, the third line leads him in turn to declare: "We—mankind—are a conversation."[62] By which he means that "the being of men" "only becomes actual in *conversation*,"[63] in the organic togetherness of their sociality. And the mission of the poet, as he contends, is that of charting out the uncertain spaces that intervene between "the gods"—that is, those primal realities and powers that stabilize and give permanence to the earth—and the people: it is he on whom they are in large part dependent for such understanding as they may win of how they are placed in the world: so Heidegger speaks of poetry as "the foundation which supports history,"[64] for it gives a ground to the "conversation," to that animating dialogue, that makes up the life of the human community. The poet is, in short, a priest of the *Polis*, and one whose magnificats validate themselves not by reason of any heterocosmic reality they summon into existence but in virtue of the sureness with which they restore to us "the ordinary universe."

Now it is of such a poet that Eliot makes a great example in our time. He is not, of course, any sort of simple case. And there are, as it must be readily admitted, many strains of emphasis in his testimony that permit a captious criticism to cite its fascination with "the still point of the turning world" as evidence that the poetry is basically controlled by intentions that are ascetical and life-denying. In one area of his mind he was, unquestionably, drawn to styles of Christian thought (as repre-

62. Heidegger, "Hölderlin and the Essence of Poetry," in *Existence and Being*, p. 301.
63. Ibid.
64. Ibid., p. 306.

sented, say, by such figures as Dame Julian and Walter Hilton and St. John of the Cross) that were not calculated to give him a firm purchase on those issues of history and *paideia* with which he was centrally preoccupied; and one wishes that, as a Catholic obedient to the English Church, he might have paid greater attention to the Caroline tradition of Anglican divinity and to such modern Anglican thinkers as Frederick Denison Maurice and Scott Holland, Charles Gore and William Temple, for, in this line, he might have found theological idioms more pat to his purpose. But, to whatever precise extent the poetry may require to be thought of as infiltrated with Platonizing and mystical impulses, it keeps as one of its major intentions the aim of dealing *politically* with the human reality: which is to say that it conceives man's place of residence to be the *Polis*, where "each living self [participates] in a common world of nature."[65] And, far from wanting to deliver human existence over to any unhistorical realm of Infinite Subjectivity, the poet of the *Quartets* wants only

> To purify the dialect of the tribe
> And urge the mind to aftersight and foresight. . . .

He wants only to remind us that "Love is the unfamiliar Name" behind the design of the *civitas terrena*. And he says that, if this City is to be like a garden with hidden waterfalls and romping children and if its people are to keep a happy rhythm in their living as in their "daunsinge"—"Holding eche other by the hand or the arm/Whiche betokenth concorde"—then a difficult choice must be made, and this the choice of a difficult path, the path (as "The Dry Salvages" calls it) of "selflessness and self-surrender" which brings us, this *via negativa*, back to "the unknown, remembered gate" leading into Blessedness and the Good Place.

So here, then, is one who elected quite a different course from that characteristically taken by the great modern poets of the Orphic way. But, in the literature of our period, it is not to Eliot alone that we must turn for a poetry of "civic virtue." In-

---

65. H. Richard Niebuhr, *The Meaning of Revelation* (New York: Macmillan Co., 1941), p. 71.

deed, it makes a small irony that he who was Eliot's bitterest antagonist in the politics of literary life, William Carlos Williams, offers another great example of such a poetry. And there are others also—Yeats from an earlier time, Frost perhaps from the recent past, Lowell in certain phases of his work, and certainly Silone and Camus among our novelists—who are committed to "the unexclusive life of the City."[66] Yet it is surely the two figures to whom we turn in the following chapters, Malraux and Auden, who are preeminent amongst those who specialize in dealing with "that common humanity whereby we are bound one to another."[67] And if, in our bewildered time, it is to imaginative literature that we are to turn for hints as to how to think about the deepest things that are in us, it may be that our first recourse should be to these Masters of the Common Journey.

66. Charles Williams, "The Redeemed City," in *The Image of the City— And Other Essays*, selected and with a critical introduction by Anne Ridler (London: Oxford University Press, 1958), p. 107.
67. The phrase is that of an eyewitness of Cranmer's martyrdom (as recorded in John Foxe's *Book of Martyrs*), quoted by Anne Ridler in her Introduction to Charles Williams's *The Image of the City*, p. xlvii.

2.

The Morality and Poetics of the City— Malraux's Definition

> "It is not by any amount of scratching at the individual that one finally comes down to mankind."
> —*The Walnut Trees of Altenburg*

> The individual stands in opposition to society, but he is nourished by it. And it is far less important to know what differentiates him than what nourishes him. —Preface to *Days of Wrath*

The assumption made by common sense about the essential pattern of the human world is that the social forms of life are contrivances that men fashion for the sake of good order and convenience when they find themselves situated in proximity to one another; and it is presumed that the individual is ontologically prior to all the various mechanisms of coexistence constituting the particular commonwealth in which he dwells. Each of us, it is supposed, is a Single One, whose reality is derived from nothing other than what the self finds to belong to the order of *mine*; and, as common sense understands the matter, the emergence of the social realm results from the individual's stepping forth, out of the integral domain of his own existence, to deal with his neighbor in the terms of fellowship and reciprocity: the world is an affair of monads choosing—or not choosing, as it may be—to join themselves to one another in community. It is such a chart of the human drama that is frequently proposed not only by unreflective reason but also by many of the decisive strategists of Western intelligence, from Aristotle to Hobbes and from Rousseau to Sartre: the "radical reality" of the human (as Ortega speaks of it)—which is *radical* because it is "of the root" and "admits of no other reality beneath it"[1]—is conceived to reside in the separate, unaccompanied person, and the body politic is thought of as originating in some kind of *contrat social.*

When, however, this traditional atomism is laid aside and when careful inquiry is undertaken into the structure of man's concrete experience, it is quite a different configuration that begins to emerge. For that primary life-world which Husserl taught European philosophy to speak of as *Lebenswelt*[2] appears, on analysis, to be one in which the primordial reality is that of men engrafted together in relations of coinherence[3]—living from and for and with their fellow men. Birth itself, as Charles Williams once reminded us, is perhaps the great "natural" symbol of that irrefragable workmanship wherewith human life is so designed as for none to be sufficient unto himself. "The man is quite helpless to produce a child unless he surrenders the means to someone else; the woman is as helpless unless she receives the means from someone else." And, as the seed fructifies and new life begins to exist, it "exists literally within its mother; it inheres in its mother."[4] Moreover, on the day the child is able for the first time to say *I*, his command of the pronoun of the first person is consequent upon his being at last able to respond to his own identity as he has found himself responded to by others: when he says *I* and thereby declares himself to be an independent center of intelligence and volition, he does so by reason of the experiences he has had of others treating him as

1. José Ortega y Gasset, *Man and People,* trans. Willard R. Trask (New York: W. W. Norton and Co., 1957), p. 38.
2. See Edmund Husserl, *The Crisis of European Sciences and Transcendental Phenomenology,* trans. David Carr (Evanston: Northwestern University Press, 1970).
3. The term is Charles Williams's and holds a central place in the design of his thought: see, for example, *The Descent of the Dove* (London: Longmans, Green and Co., 1939), *He Came Down from Heaven* (London: Faber and Faber, 1940), and *The Image of the City* (London–New York: Oxford University Press, 1958).
4. *The Image of the City,* p. 150.

indeed *another*: he sees himself as seen, hears himself as heard, speaks to himself as spoken to.[5]

And so it is throughout the length and breadth of man's world: the human reality is everywhere that of our being "members one of another," of our lives being enveloped within relations of responsiveness and interaction with our brethren, so much so indeed that, from one standpoint perhaps, the "ontological difference"[6] represented by the human creature is definable simply as *fellowmanhood*. Just as the child first learns to say *I* only in relation to *you*, so is the entirety of personal existence carried out in relation to *others*. Which is what gives cogency to the late Richard Niebuhr's contention that the image of man-the-answerer is more fully evocative of our "lived" world than the older images of man-the-maker and man-the-citizen.[7] For the pattern of all that we do and are is formed by the exigencies arising out of our dialogical commitments—"to answer questions addressed to us, to defend ourselves against attacks, to reply to injunctions, to meet challenges. . . ."[8] No man is an island, and the whole emphasis of our thought and feeling and action represents a response to the ways in which our lives are touched by the various social matrices to which we belong. We are not, of course, merely epiphenomena of Social Process; and, over and again in the round of human affairs, when men find themselves confronting collectivities that impose an alien and oppressive order, it seems needful to launch campaigns of resistance against the Leviathan, against whatever array of power and authority it may be in the public world that threatens some intolerable infringement of freedom and dignity. Yet, however much the exactions of authenticity may occasionally require man to become (in Camus' phrase) *l'homme révolté*, he remains a creature the essential structure of whose life requires him to

5. See H. Richard Niebuhr, *The Responsible Self* (New York: Harper and Row, 1963), p. 72: "To be a being that is an object to itself is possible genetically and actually only as I . . . see myself as seen, hear myself as heard, speak to myself as spoken to."

6. The phrase "ontological difference" is Martin Heidegger's: it occurs in many of his writings but was first employed in his essay of 1929, *Vom Wesen des Grundes* (Halle: Niemeyer).

7. H. Richard Niebuhr, *The Responsible Self*, pp. 48–60.

8. Ibid., p. 56.

say, "The world is a wedding"—since, everywhere, the horizon encompassing all his plans and projects is one that discloses each mortal soul to be a "peece of the Continent, a part of the maine," and this to so profound a degree as to give a kind of heraldic rank to the words of St. Anthony of Egypt, "Your life and your death are with your neighbor."

Under such a perspective and within the terms of our modern parlance, the proper name for the scene of human life is the City. The ancient metropolis—in Athens, Jerusalem, Rome, Alexandria —exhibited, of course, often very impressively, the phenomenon of interdependence, and its industry and commerce and intellectual enterprise entailed an elaborate network of cultural transaction. But its modes of exchange, even when highly developed, will inevitably seem rudimentary when thought of in relation to the incredibly complicated machinery of provision for men's needs made necessary by the huge aggregations of life embraced by the great urban centers of our time. For here, in the massive communities presented today by Chicago and New York and London and Paris, nothing resembling a civilized society would be possible, manifestly, apart from systems of cooperation infinitely more complex than any polity that could have been dreamt of two centuries ago (not to speak of two thousand years ago). The modern metropolis is, of course, a vast society of "employees"—of managers and clerks, of proletarians and technicians and professionals—each of whom is attached to a certain job. And this job—whether it be the reading of gas meters or the repairing of automobiles or the cleaning of streets or the practice of medicine—must be performed efficiently and punctually, if there is not to be serious breakdown in the total system of a community's life. True, we are not involved in any personal relationship with our supermarket checker and garage mechanic and bank clerk, and the residents of Boston and Detroit undoubtedly have a far more restricted range of "primary" relationships than men had in the towns and villages of an earlier time. But modern urbanites are dependent on a far more highly diversified body of people for the satisfaction of their daily needs than earlier systems of life required. The unseen telephone operator, the unseen technician controlling the check-processing computer in one's local bank, the unseen medical technologist handling a sample of one's blood in a hospital laboratory, the unseen truck driver making his delivery of foodstuffs each morning to one's neighborhood grocer, the unseen corps of workers supervising the electrical and the water systems of a large metropolitan area—on all these and on thousands of others we are constantly dependent for our safety and comfort and peace. So the City, then, is the name not only for a certain kind of sociological reality but also, and more profoundly, for the human world in the dimension of its unity and interdependence, of its answerability to the law of Coinherence. The City is, in short, the name of the human community—in its oneness and indivisibility.

Its moralists in the modern period are, of course, numerous, and they comprise a highly various company. Yet whether one turns to Max Scheler's doctrine of *Sympathie*[9] or to Martin Buber's doctrine of "dialogue,"[10] to Gabriel Marcel's themes of "presence" and "fidelity"[11] or to Camus' doctrine of *mesure*,[12] or to Dietrich Bonhoeffer's doctrine of "deputyship,"[13] one discovers these thinkers and innumerable others to be declaring in effect that the City finds its health and equanimity and its supreme ordinance in what Charles Williams liked always to denominate as Exchange—which was for him but the discipline whereby men seek in their commerce with one another to acknowledge the Coinherence of all life. Williams's very radical commitment as an Anglican to the legacies of Catholic theology made it

9. See Max Scheler, *Wesen und Formen der Sympathie* (Bonn: Cohen, 1923).

10. See Martin Buber, *I and Thou,* trans. Ronald Gregor Smith (Edinburgh: T. & T. Clark, 1937); *Between Man and Man,* trans. Ronald Gregor Smith (New York: Macmillan Co., 1948); and *The Knowledge of Man,* trans. Maurice Friedman and Ronald Gregor Smith (New York: Harper and Row, 1965).

11. See Gabriel Marcel, *The Mystery of Being,* vol. I, trans. G. S. Fraser, and vol. II, trans. René Hague (Chicago: Henry Regnery Co., 1951); *Creative Fidelity,* trans. Robert Rosthal (New York: Farrar, Straus, 1964); and *Tragic Wisdom and Beyond,* trans. Stephen Jolin and Peter McCormick (Evanston: Northwestern University Press, 1973).

12. See Albert Camus, *L'Homme révolté* (Paris: Gallimard, 1951).

13. See Dietrich Bonhoeffer, *Ethics,* trans. Neville Horton Smith (New York: Macmillan Co., 1955).

natural for him to find the paradigmatic instance and ultimate source of all the coinherent relations of the world in that mysterious circumincession whereby the three coequal Hypostases of the Holy Trinity eternally inhere in one another. But, in the exposition of his thought set forth in his great book *He Came Down from Heaven,* he is at pains to insist that, though the principle of Coinherence may need ultimately to be understood in relation to the doctrine of Glory, it does nevertheless speak about a "natural" fact of existence, a *res publica,* the first apprehension of which does not immediately necessitate any supernatural reference. For Nature so replicates Supernature that, everywhere, Coinherence (with its correlative discipline of Exchange) diagrams the way in which the human City operates: it is the very "inscape" of our hearts and of all societies, since "no man lives to himself or . . . *from* himself."[14] "The name of the City is Union. . . . The process of that union is by the method of free exchange."[15] There would in fact be no life at all, were it not for that exchange "between the father and mother which results in the transference of seed."[16] And the principle expressed in marriage and childbirth is that which is implicit in all the myriad arrangements between men that make the human enterprise possible. Some teach and some heal, some sow and some reap; some labor at furnaces or in the depths of the earth, while still others rule or employ or keep the hearth; some toil by day and some by night. The City, in other words, is an organism, and survives only by way of "diversities of ministrations." Which is to say that Williams's lesson is St. Paul's, that the foot may not quarrel because it is not the hand or the ear because it is not the eye, for all the members are set within the body and are "tempered . . . together," so that if "one member suffereth, all the members suffer with it" (1 Corinthians 12:4–26).

Or, to put the issue in the terms Williams would seem most to have preferred, the City functions only in the degree to which we consent to "bear one another's burdens." And his appellative for this basic *quid pro quo* of the moral life is Substitution, for

14. Williams, *The Image of the City,* p. 104.
15. Ibid., p. 103.
16. Ibid.

it is precisely a kind of intermutation that he conceives the bearing of burdens most essentially to entail. Burdens are sometimes onerous and sometimes negligible, but, heavy or light, if they surpass our powers of endurance or our capacity for coping, our carrying on will depend on cares being lifted and on their then being borne by another. "A" hands over to "B" the burdens with which he cannot deal: "B" consents to stand in his stead, and can manage to do so because the unmanageable burdens of his own are borne by yet another—this is the way Exchange works. It is, says a character in Williams's novel *Descent into Hell*, like " 'taking in each other's washing.' " This personage, Pauline Anstruther, at a certain crucial moment, before she is persuaded to submit to the logic of Substitution, says to her friend, the poet Peter Stanhope—with a touch of indignation, at the thought of herself troubling another—" 'Would I push my burden on to anybody else?' " To which Stanhope replies:

> "Not if you insist on making a universe for yourself. . . . If you want to disobey and refuse the laws that are common to us all, if you want to live in pride and division and anger, you can. But if you will be part of the best of us, and live and laugh and be ashamed with us, then you must be content to be helped. You must give your burden up to someone else, and you must carry someone else's burden. I haven't made the universe and it isn't my fault. But I'm sure that this is a law of the universe, and not to give up your parcel is as much to rebel as not to carry another's. . . ."[17]

We are, in short, "members one of another": we are one another's *limbs*—and, given the Coinherence into which all life is gathered up, the fundamental law of the City is, therefore, that of Substitution and Exchange. This is the declaration of Charles Williams, as it is also in essence that of many of the great moralists of the modern period who have reflected most deeply on the nature of civic virtue.

Yet, in that *Gestalt* of grace wherein the City finds its enabling principle, there is a further element to be remarked, for if "life

17. Charles Williams, *Descent into Hell* (Grand Rapids, Mich.: Wm. B. Eerdmans, n.d.), p. 99; used by permission.

together" is an affair of Substitution and Exchange, then it must be conceived to involve most essentially a kind of sacrificial discipline. For when we act *for* others—as when a "father acts for the children, working for them, caring for them, interceding, fighting and suffering for them" and thus undertaking to be "their deputy"[18]—something is being given up; life is *releasing* itself as an offering to other life: that which is of one's own is being handed over to another, for the sake of the human communion—and this *leitourgia* has the character of a sacrificial service. But though a richly detailed anatomy of what is here at stake will be found available in the testimony that has come in our time from the great moralists of the City, it is a striking fact of modern literature that it presents only very rarely any large poetic account of Substitution, of Exchange, of Sacrifice. Given the size and complexity of the issue, the particular forms of poetic art that one naturally counts on for salient explorations in this regard are the novel and the drama, for here, where the powers of men are engaged at full stretch, we expect, far more so perhaps than in the modes of lyric poetry, to be overtaken by "the reek of the human."[19] Yet what one actually encounters is a strange silence about those realities of Exchange and Sacrifice that constitute the central human discipline. In the drama of our period, apart from the demure mystifications of Eliot's *Cocktail Party* and the extraordinary images of *Freundlichkeit* that occasionally bring a sudden and surprising radiance onto the stage of Bertolt Brecht (as in *The Trial of Lucullus*, or *The Good Woman of Setzuan*), there is little to be cited in the way of impressive examples of Substitution in modern theatre. And, in the literature of prose fiction, one will think perhaps of those deeply affecting "moralities" that Ignazio Silone was producing a generation ago and of the examples they offer—in *Fontamara* (1930), *Bread and Wine* (1937), *The Seed Beneath the Snow* (1940)—of a Berardo Viola or a Pietro Spina undertaking the burdens of a vocation toward a "secular" sanctity of reverence

18. Dietrich Bonhoeffer, *Ethics*, p. 194.

19. The phrase is Donald Davies': see his *Articulate Energy: An Enquiry into the Syntax of English Poetry* (New York: Harcourt, Brace and Co., 1958), p. 161.

for "the sacrament of the brother."[20] Or one may think of the unhappy martyrs who carry out that dialectic of redemption in which some of Graham Greene's strange fables are grounded (say, *The Power and the Glory* or *The Heart of the Matter*). Or, again, the English critic Raymond Williams is convinced— though not persuasively so—that Boris Pasternak's moving book of 1957, *Doctor Zhivago*, records a drama which is in a great way focalized by "a sacrifice of life for life."[21] And no doubt some few other equally problematical examples may be summoned forth, but, generally, the modern novel has specialized in the dreary, hapless themes of absurdity and alienation and shipwreck: as a friend of mine (who is one of the most gifted younger American novelists of the present time) said to me, with an ironically resigned shrug of the shoulder, when I asked him if he could think of one indubitably great novel of the past fifty years that dramatizes in some large way the issues of Substitution and Exchange, "Sydney Carton est mort."

Indeed: the human style of the hero of *A Tale of Two Cities* is very probably not something easily recoverable in the literary ethos of our own present. For the imagination of Substitution and Sacrifice becomes possible only when it can be supposed that the self, in confronting the unvoiced plea of another for comfort and succor and deliverance, is being "spoken to" and "addressed" by a presence whose dignity surpasses that which might be conceived to belong merely to the particular individual who happens to be suffering some acute insolvency. If the "I," in meeting the "Thou," meets only another human being, finite and no less imperfect than himself, then the "I" is unlikely to be powerfully moved to invest itself in any great way in the "Thou," no matter how piteously this latter's condition may be calculated to touch the heart. On the contrary: in the drama of human dialogue, it is only when some great silent partner is felt to be so involved in the reality of the "Thou" as to make the claims he exerts on the "I" in effect a *word* spoken to the "I" by an *eternal* Thou in

20. The phrase is Hans Urs von Balthasar's: see his *Science, Religion and Christianity,* trans. Hilda Graef (Westminster, Md.: Newman Press, 1958), pp. 142–55.
21. See Raymond Williams, *Modern Tragedy* (Stanford, Calif.: Stanford University Press, 1966), pp. 167–73.

whom the "I" itself is implicated—it is only then, when the human image is experienced as in some sort a *sacramentum gloriae*, that the possibility of life being laid down in behalf of other life can be deeply felt. And it is, of course, precisely this sacramentalist view of the human reality which is at a great discount in a culture so thoroughly secularized as our own, where the wise men of the age are prepared to think of us as material for one or another kind of engineering but are quite unprepared to adduce compelling metaphysical justification of the sacredness of the person. So it ought not to be considered surprising that the literature of this century rarely presents great examples of men undertaking those special disciplines wherewith the life of the City is given its main chance.

When, under the sign of the *désacralisé*, the literary imagination does undertake to celebrate what Silone calls "the intimate reality of others," it may be expected to do so uncertainly and falteringly, and its affirmations—as in the fiction of Camus or the theatre of Brecht—will be experimental and more than a little gratuitous. Yet these are the tenuities within the terms of which the search must be carried on for such quickening traces as our literature proffers of what it is like to pay homage to "the sacrament of the brother." And, in this somewhat diminished context, it is the fiction of André Malraux that, in its exemplary devotion to the evangel of *fraternité*, has remained over the past generation as one of the great testimonies of the age.

This *haut aventurier*, in the well-nigh unexampled breadth and diversity of his experience, has commanded a kind of vantage in relation to the modern landscape such as few writers of this century have enjoyed. Indeed, the career is one of the absolute astonishments of our time. In October of 1923, when not yet quite twenty-two years of age, he plunged into unexplored tracts of Cambodian jungle in the neighborhood of Angkor Wat to search for lost treasures of Khmer art, and did in fact discover a hoard in the ruined temple at Banteay Srei. But then his mistaken assumption that he was free to remove the sculptures he had found led to his arrest, to charges being preferred by the French colonial administration, and to protracted litigations. The final outcome, however, in October of

1924 was nothing more serious (partly because of intercessions on his behalf by many leading French writers) than a suspended sentence of a year's imprisonment. After his return to France, in January 1925, he was again in Indochina, founding in June of that year in Saigon a newspaper (*L'Indochine*) dedicated to radical indictments of the French colonial bureaucracy. By the end of the summer the government had bullied his publisher into withdrawing support of the enterprise, and thus, with the help of Annamite friends, he established in November another paper—*L'Indochine Enchaînée*—which, again, was unable at last to survive government interference. Through the late twenties and early thirties he was traveling to the Soviet Union, to China and India, and moving in and out of Persia and Afghanistan. In the spring of 1934 he was publishing a series of articles in the Parisian newspaper *L'Intransigeant* on his discovery a few weeks earlier by plane in the region of Mar'ib over the Arabian desert of the ruins of the lost city of the Queen of Sheba, the capital of the old Sabaean civilization. By this time he was being widely recognized as a leading figure in leftist intellectual circles in France, and thus he was one of the main European delegates at the Congress of Soviet Writers in the summer of '34 and played a key role in organizing the International Congress in Defense of Culture the following spring. After the outbreak of the Spanish War in July 1936, he fought on the Loyalist side as the commander of an heroic air squadron, and, in battered old crates, he flew at great odds in sixty-five missions. In the Second World War he fought in the French Army's tank corps, and, after the fall of France, under the *nom de guerre* Berger became a legend in the Resistance movement (as a colonel among the *maquisards*) and in General Leclerc's Army of Liberation in Alsace (as a brigade commander). In the postwar period he was (as he is today) one of the most influential senior editors on the staff of the great publishing house of Gallimard, where one of his numerous projects has been the direction of the distinguished series of art books which the firm calls *La Galerie de la Pléiade*. For more than a decade, from 1958 to 1969, he served in the DeGaulle government, first as Minister of Information and then as *Ministre d'État chargé des Affaires*

Culturelles. And across this long stretch of years, lived always in the public realm at an extraordinary pitch of intensity (from that first youthful foray into Indochina even unto the present time), Malraux has produced—in his novels and in his famous books on the history of art—a body of work that stands as one of the decisive monuments of the literary world of this century.

The author of *La Condition humaine,* of *L'Espoir,* of *Les Noyers de l'Altenburg,* or of *La Psychologie de l'art* and *Les Voix du silence* will, of course, conventionally be thought of as a novelist and as at once a theorist and an historian of art. But perhaps the more appropriate view is one that considers him, in all his diverse literary accomplishment—whether in the field of fiction or autobiography or art criticism—as having most essentially enacted something like the role of poet. The special kind of theatricality, for example, that marks the novels would seem to be the result of their having been shaped by a basically poetic procedure. Nowhere in his work do we encounter that particular density of texture which, as it follows from a gossipy anecdotalism about chains of highly personalized event, distinguishes —in, say, *Emma* or *The Possessed* or *The Magic Mountain* or *Light in August*—the great normative instances of modern prose fiction. Instead, in *Man's Fate* (*La Condition humaine*) or in *Man's Hope* (*L'Espoir*) or in *The Walnut Trees of Altenburg* (*Les Noyers de l'Altenburg*), we encounter a suite of images whose brilliant *montage* largely carries the given occasion: the controlling impresario is a kind of cinematographer who so carefully arranges a series of episodes as to make "the individual fragments exist as 'stills' "[22] or as an artfully disposed structure of snapshots which quite thoroughly suspends conventional expectations of the *reportage* (of great masses of fact) that the novelistic chronicle normally provides. Or, again, those who have paid the closest attention to Malraux's books on art, however deeply they may be affected by the dazzling torrent of eloquence with which he deploys his immense learning, are often to be found disinclined to think of these works in the established terms either of art history or of philosophical aesthetic: they are

22. William Righter, *The Rhetorical Hero: An Essay on the Aesthetics of André Malraux* (London: Routledge and Kegan Paul, 1964), p. 9.

rather felt to be vast doxologies which want to celebrate the metamorphosing powers of the human spirit evidenced by the history of art, and to hold them up as pledge and proof that, for all the fatalities of nature and history, a kind of transcendence is finally possible. In short, this prodigiously intelligent "witness" of the Human Condition shows himself again and again, in the books that constitute the central statements of his career, to be one the main burden of whose meditation very much represents a mode of poetic vision.

Nor is Malraux's poetry unrelated to that fearful sense of man's ultimate insecurity by which so much of modern literature is stricken. Indeed, his first published work of any consequence, the surrealistic fable of 1921 called *Lunes en papier*, takes us into a *royaume farfelu*. Nine strange little half-men set out on an expedition in search of Death, whom they intend to assassinate. And, after an arduous journey through a heavily forested country replete with fantastic and threatening monsters, they do at last enter the precincts of Death's own kingdom—only to find, however, that Death is already desperately ill and has been contemplating suicide. So miserable is she in fact that, after bathing in a special solution prescribed by her physician and finding it to be an acid mortally corrosive of her aluminum skeleton, she raises not a murmur of protest and dies contentedly —but not before her physician is unmasked and revealed to be of the party of assassins. Then, after she has expired, they look at one another with bafflement and futilely try to remember why it was that they had wanted to destroy her. The fable is quite the sort of *divertissement* a very young writer might have been expected to turn out in the France of Max Jacob and Blaise Cendrars, of Léon-Paul Fargue and André Breton. But, for all its quirky whimsicality, when it is viewed in relation to the course that his writing was subsequently to take, what may seem most significant perhaps in this first venture is the inclination it reflects in the young Malraux to locate the scene and site of our ultimate contentions in the realm of the *farfelu*, of the bizarre and the grotesque and the Wholly Other. And it is manifestly a similar emphasis that was shaping the various fragments of narrative that he occasionally published in French journals through the 1920s (materials presumably intended for an unrealized book to have been called *Ecrits pour une idole à trompe*) —as it was also much the same point of view controlling the elaborately fantastical tale entitled *Royaume farfelu* that Gallimard issued in 1928. So, given this early sense of the real center of interest in the human story being possibly Elsewhere, we should no doubt not be greatly startled by the fact that in Malraux's first major work, the book of 1926 called *La Tentation de l'occident* (*The Temptation of the West*), the most striking sentence of all is that which says, by way of Malraux's own italics: ". . . *at the center of European man, dominating the great movements of his life, there resides an essential absurdity.*"

The Temptation of the West is a small book which simply stitches together a series of imaginary letters exchanged between two young men in the midst of their travels—between Ling, a Chinese tourist on the European continent, and A.D., his French correspondent who is visiting China. Both are deeply impressed by what they feel to be the immense distance separating the spiritual universe of the modern West from that of the Orient, and their letters to each other—in terms not unlike those of Nietzsche and Spengler and Keyserling—are largely given over to an attempt at defining their sense of the absolute difference presented by the two cultures. Unlike Chinese spirituality which is captured by a sense of the pure objectivity of the universe and of the subordinacy of the human self with respect to Things, which is primarily fascinated indeed by the marvelous *élan* and fecundity wherewith Things are carried along in their flow through ceaseless births and renewals—unlike this Oriental veneration of the infranatural vitality that subsumes the whole of existence and that in effect asks man for a kind of deference toward the unceasing entreaties of the world, the fundamental datum of Western sensibility is conceived by these two young men to be that of the self standing over against the not-self and seeking ways of imposing on the earth a human meaning. As Ling says in one of his letters to A.D., "Time is what *you* make it; we are what it makes us." And the young Frenchman is not at all inclined to burke the charge, for he also thinks of the distinctively Western point of view as one representing a resolve to make the world obedient to human intentionality: the people of the Occident are constantly drunk with their own goals, they think of man as having been given dominion over Creation, the universe they look out upon is one meant to be submissive to the human will, and thus they are dedicated above all else to a life of action.

Now this great passion for mastering the world and making it subservient to the human project is felt by both Ling and A.D. to be undoubtedly the source of the extraordinary dynamism of Western culture, of its unexampled genius for shaping the course of nature and history and for facing in a hopeful way the horizon of the future. Yet, for all the creativeness that may be a part of this intensity, it involves, as they conclude, a dialectic that carries within itself a sad kind of irony. For the habit of imagination whereby man and the world are conceived to represent such a duality as tends to encourage his approaching it in a spirit of assertiveness and aggression did, from the very beginning, spell something like doom for the Christian dispensation, since, when the world is thought of as only so much inert material awaiting the impress of human purposiveness, it is inevitably experienced as something silent and untouched by any kind of sacramentality. But not only is the light of Heaven bound to be extinguished finally by Western voluntarism: in a strange way, the death of God entails also the death of Man. When the world is everywhere besmudged by man's volitionality and when no sheer *other*ness can anywhere be easily descried, the resulting ennui of the human brings at last a kind of nihilism that undermines even the dignity of *la présence humaine*. And the result, in Ling's phrase, is *une absurdité essentielle*.

So it was that Malraux's meditation proceeded in the book of 1926, and a similar preoccupation with the radical absurdity invading the Western world is also very much at the center of the famous essay entitled *D'une jeunesse européenne* ("On European Youth") that he published in the following year in what was to be the final volume of *Les Cahiers verts*. Here, his primary assumption is that, given the insolvency now of those Christian premises on which the whole Western venture has been reared, the great necessity facing the young is that of "creating a new reality," of building a new conception of man. But, in a time when the terrible logic set afoot by the death of God ineluctably devolves into an eclipse of the human image itself (and thus of the ground whereon genuine community may be sought), the prevalent condition proves to be one of men's being so jailed into the solipsistic isolation of the individual ego as to be unable to recover any lively sense of their generic nature. And since it is precisely this subjectivistic individualism which has fed that will to will and that inordinate propensity for action whereby the Western enterprise has been undone, we are thus, in the analysis of the *D'une jeunesse* essay, doubled back upon the horns of our most fundamental dilemma, so much so as to have led this young diagnostician to suggest that "if Nietzsche finds so many echoes in despairing hearts, it is because he is himself only the expression of their despair. . . ."

Indeed, there is perhaps no sentence in the essay of 1927 more revealing of Malraux's stringency than that which says: "Lacking a doctrine, [the young European] has nothing left but a resolute will to give battle." *The Temptation of the West,* however, is asserting that it is just this, the will to give battle, which has broken those great covenants between man and the world bequeathed by the Christian centuries, since it is the inveterate imperialism and manipulativeness with which Occidental people have handled the things of earth that, inevitably, have had the effect, as it were, of casting the world under the sign of the *désacralisé.* What makes the exchanges between Ling and A.D. so notable is precisely the distinctness with which they are registering their mistrust of that cult of action to which they believe Western mentality is incorrigibly committed, and, in this regard, theirs is an apprehension that would seem indeed to have been Malraux's. Yet so deprived of alternatives does the author of *D'une jeunesse européenne* consider the post-Christian man to be that, at last, he appears unable to envisage any other course for the young European—amidst all the sad divestments of this late time—than that of "a resolute will to give battle." Which would seem in fact tantamount to the proposal of a kind of *mauvaise foi* as the one remaining basis for the conduct of life at the end of the modern age.

It is, then, a very desperate route indeed being described in the late 1920s by Malraux's movement—from the essays (*The Temptation of the West* and *D'une jeunesse européenne*) expressing a profound disbelief in action to the novels appearing towards the end of the decade which, nevertheless, are holding forth a bold kind of enterprise in extreme situations as emblematic of a truly human authenticity. Yet it was such a route that was being traversed by the author of *Les Conquérants* (*The Conquerors*), published by Grasset in 1928, and *La Voie royale* (*The Royal Way*), published by the same firm in 1930, for both these novels conceive it to be the case that the great thing is (as it is said in *The Conquerors*) "to concentrate one's mind on some great action, to pursue it, to be haunted, to be intoxicated by the thought of it. . . ."

The fictitiousness of the old legend about Malraux's having been a member of the Kuomintang's Committee of Twelve in the late twenties has long since been established. But, even so, it is apparent that his frequent contact as a young man with the Far East had led him to take a profound interest in the revolutionary Chinese insurgency of the period, and the general strike organized by the Nationalists in the summer of 1925 in Canton (as a blow against British shipping interests centered at Hong Kong, by the mouth of the Canton River) forms the background of *The Conquerors*—just as the essential material which is dramatized in *The Royal Way* derives from Malraux's Indochinese expedition of 1923 and '24 in search of Khmerian statuary.

The book of 1928, in the swift syncopation of its scenic development, presents the first major example in Malraux's writing of his affinity—as a poet of the novel—for the cinematic modes of fiction. We are hurtled along from one circumstance to another by a language so brisk that its curt telegraphy often very nearly dispenses altogether with conventional syntax, in its eagerness to plunge us into the absoluteness of the event. The unnamed narrator who speaks in the first person constantly prefers the present tense; and, in a manner resembling the styles of *montage* in Dos Passos' *U.S.A.* trilogy, Malraux occasionally intersperses his fragments of narrative and conversation with newspaper headlines and snippets of wireless bulletins—a procedure, again, calculated by this cinematographer to induce a sense of immersion within the torrential onrush of happenings and emergencies, a sense of the absoluteness of History.

At the center of the stage is one Pierre Garine, an exile from his native Switzerland, whose experience of the world has convinced him that the established protocols of human society not only legitimize injustice but also, more fundamentally, entail— in their utter gratuitousness—a totally uncreditable kind of absurdity. "No social order," he says, "is anything to me." And yet, though the human world strikes him as something like a grimace one sees in a distorting mirror, he considers that, for all its vanity and futility, one may not live *in* that vanity: some response, some rejoinder, must be flung back at it—some audacious and intrepid *non serviam* must be spoken out against the Absurd. So he finds his calling in "dedication to a great action," for this alone, as he decides, is the course that offers some chance of one's leaving a scar on the map of history. He comes out to the Orient to join the advancing movement of Chinese nationalism that Sun Yat-sen had launched: here, he thinks, he may at last win the opportunity for the decisive *coup,* for the great deed. And thus, in the summer of 1925, amidst the furious guerrilla skirmishing brought by the general strike in Canton, we find him building an intelligence and propaganda apparatus in the city for the Kuomintang and playing a central role in the whole uprising.

But for this unhappy man there is no clear path leading out of the blind alleys of the world. For the Chinese Nationalists, having been unable to gain any support for their movement in Western quarters, have had to turn to Russia for assistance. And Garine knows that, once a revolutionary movement begins to be the creature of the Comintern, there can be no room left in it for one like himself who has never learned to "obey." Over a long period, though ravaged by fever and dysentery, he has not permitted himself to be deflected from his commitment to the revolution by his steadily worsening health: despite his declining strength, he has remained steadfast in his determination to see this effort through to its finish, since, as he says, "There is but one thing that matters in life: not to be conquered"—*ne pas être vaincu.* Yet at last there seems to be no possibility of staving off the Absurd. He is so ruined by malaria and dysentery that he knows death to be not far off. And, even could he somehow be rescued from the infirmities of his body, he knows that in the end there would be no prospect of any fulfillment in revolutionary enterprise, since, once that enterprise is crowned with success, its regents will consolidate their gains by methods absolutely opposed to those whereby they won their victory: which is to say that they will be unprepared to tolerate such a nonconformist as himself. In short, he knows that his day is over: "I have not cast off the dust of Europe from my feet . . . to come here either to teach or to learn the word 'obedience.' " Thus the clangor made by the Red Army's approaching Canton—"almost metallic, like . . . the rhythmic fall of hammers"—carries for him, in its strident discordancy, a sound knelling his own defeat.

Now it is essentially this same anecdote which is being re-counted in *The Royal Way,* the novel that Malraux published two years after the appearance of *The Conquerors.* True, the setting is that not of a great Chinese metropolis but of the jungle regions of Cambodia along the ancient Khmer Royal Road, and the project to which the central personages of the novel are committed is that not of organizing a strike and launching a revolu-tion but rather that of pillaging ruined Khmer temples of their treasures of statuary. Yet, as regards the more commanding figure of the two principals, the spiritual drama being enacted re-mains (as in *The Conquerors*) that of an unhappy *isolé* who seeks deliverance from despair in *le combat décisif* of adventure itself but who, like Garine, does at last find himself so hopelessly impaled on the world's absurdity that not even "lucidity" offers any genuine transcendence.

The young French archaeologist, Claude Vannec, on his way out to the Far East meets on board his ship an older man who has become already something of a scandalous legend, one Perken, a displaced European now on his uppers, who has "re-fused to live in the community of men," pursuing instead a career as soldier of fortune in various backwaters of the Orient, where indeed he has lately (in the manner of Conrad's Kurtz) presided over a kingdom of his own in the remote fastnesses of the Thailand interior, hoping that at least here he may "leave a scar on the map." "Just to *be* a king," he says, "means nothing; it's the building up of a kingdom that's worth while." And his great ambition now is to secure money enough to arm his tribesmen, so that he may broadly extend his reign throughout the Siamese interior and in this way make certain that the map will not be unscarred by his own passion for dominion. Vannec, on the other hand, is a young intellectual, an Orientalist well versed in the *trouvaille* that may be assumed to be hidden in the deserted temples along Cambodia's Royal Road; and, since he is without any independency of means and has no intention of choosing "between eating in bargain restaurants and selling autos," he, in the spirit of a gambler, has decided to search out this treasure trove of Khmerian art, to remove as much of it as he can from the country, and sell it to the highest bidder. These two, Perken and Vannec, strike up an acquaintance on board the ship carrying them to Singapore, and, in due course, after Vannec invites Perken to join forces with him on a basis of full partnership in the sharing of the spoils, the older man accepts the proposal, both being confident that a quick fortune awaits them.

So, after their ship lands at Singapore, though Perken must proceed on immediately to Bangkok and Vannec must go to Saigon for accreditation by the French colonial authorities, they are agreed that they will rejoin each other at Pnom-Penh, and so they do a few weeks later, setting out from thence for Siem-Reap, from which with their gear and native retainers they plunge into the jungled interior. The line of the Royal Road, however, is well-nigh obliterated by the bush and slime of these fearfully repellent wilds, and the journey proves to be arduous beyond even Vannec's darkest forebodings. They do, indeed, eventually discover the moldering temples Vannec had reckoned on, but no sooner have they managed with their hammers and chisels to dislodge with great difficulty the most beautiful of the bas-reliefs and to load their carts than they are then deserted by their native guides and cartmen. Deeming it imprudent to try by themselves to retrace their route, they strike out northward into the highlands of the half-savage Stieng people, thinking that their only chance of success lies in pushing on to Siam, from whence their hoard may be shipped back to Europe. And, for Perken, this course has the advantage of giving him an opportunity to scout out the whereabouts of Grabot, like himself a European adventurer who has won suzerainty over a vast native populace somewhere in the Cambodian bush and whom Perken sullenly regards as a possibly threatening rival. Nor is the overtaking of Grabot long postponed, for, in the first native village they come to, they find this hapless man, now horribly broken and mutilated by his captors who are of the Moi tribe: he is kept harnessed to a treadmill, and has been so cudgeled and maimed as to have become a kind of half-demented animal in whom there is hardly the trace of any residual humanity to be descried. Perken and Vannec assume that theirs may be a similar fate at the hands of these fierce Moi tribesmen, but they do finally persuade the chiefs to allow them to continue on to Siam for trinketry with which to purchase Grabot's release. Before taking their departure, however, Perken, in walking across the compound, stumbles on a war-spike planted in the ground and badly wounds his knee, so badly in fact that by the time he and Vannec have reached the Siamese border the knee has become gangrenous; and he is bluntly told by an English doctor that, since there is no hospital in the neighborhood where an amputation could be performed, he will be dead in a fortnight. Under this doomful sentence, he resolves to return to his own "kingdom" in the north, and Vannec undertakes to get him there; but, before the territory can be reached, he dies—in Vannec's arms, the two held together in a "desperate fraternity."

Thus it is that this adversary of the Absurd is at last surmounted by that ultimate and inescapable affliction whose sign is the skull and crossbones. Like Garine in *The Conquerors*, Perken also is one who no longer sleeps in the old myths of the Greeks and the Jews and who, in the spirit of a cool objectivity, confronts that yawning emptiness in the world which says in effect that a man's life wins importance in the degree to which he addresses it as a project for which he alone is responsible. Amidst the environing voids (both social-historical and metaphysical), a man's only chance of redeeming himself from insignificance lies in *le combat décisif,* in a great act of will whereby on the map of things at least some scar may be left as a result of his sojourning on the earth: so, as Garine had thrown in with the nascent Kuomintang, Perken makes his stand (against the jungles of Siam, as well as against the European scene from which he has expatriated himself) by instituting his own principality and power—and both his jungle in Thailand and those wild Cambodian tracts into which he and Vannec plunge in search of treasure are intended by the novel to be, in the recalcitrance that their many perils offer to the human endeavor, an image of the massive hazardousness that the world everywhere presents. And though in the sequestered domain of his sovereignty in the Thai uplands Perken may impose some semblance of order on the tangled thickets of life in these Far Eastern wilds, his small victory proves finally to be of the hollowest kind. For there is in the end no escaping the *maîtresse de la forêt:* which is to say that his finitude leaves him ultimately at the mercy of disease and death, and thus unable to ward off that cruelest stroke of the Absurd—which is beyond remedy.

Yet, though the melodrama of *The Royal Way* ends (with Perken's death) in a defeat as absolute as that in which *The Conquerors* culminates, the novel of 1930 may, nevertheless, be felt to mark the end of one phase of Malraux's development and to look toward another. It is, to be sure, deeply informed by the kind of distressed preoccupation with general anarchy that unifies his early work, and, like *The Conquerors,* it finds the human norm in an embattled resolve, through boldness of enterprise, to impose significance and order on at least some limited quarter of the world. But *The Royal Way* is finally reaching beyond the mystique of *action* to the great theme being adumbrated in the central books of Malraux's career as a novelist, for, notwithstanding the universal reign of absurdity, it does at last want, however tentatively, to envisage a consolatory grace in the reality of human communion itself. True, amidst the empty inertia of the world, Perken can find no evidence of any ontological confirmation or support of human existence; and the novel offers his final defenselessness before the utter extinction brought by death as an example of the immolation which is reserved by the Absurd as man's ultimate destiny. Yet, broken and battered though his last state is, in that anxious race northward at the end, he is at least not deserted by his comrade Vannec. As he bitterly contemplates how the world has strangled "the little nucleus of hopes that was his . . . life" and as his mind is reeled by the spasms of excruciating pain that seize him on his litter, he feels intermittently something of that resentment toward Vannec that it is natural for the dying to feel toward those who will continue to walk upon the earth after they are gone. But, even so, they have had their common endeavor, their joint effort: they have struggled together against the jungle and been upborne by their bond of loyalty to each other, and thus in Perken's last hour, as Vannec holds the tortured man in his arms, their "desperate fraternity" confers a kind of fragile shelter against tribulation.

It is, of course, a very private moment in which Perken and Vannec are granted their uncertain transfiguration: they are both men who feel themselves to have been badgered into refusing "to live in the community of men," and what they have together, in a remote and desolate corner of the earth, is a matter of an utterly isolated duet that does not appear to carry any implication for the general world of humankind. But, when their little drama is considered with respect to the more richly variegated material that Malraux was to be organizing in his later books, it may be felt to be pointing towards the lesson being laid down there regarding the larger relations of the human City—that, as it is said in *Le Temps du mépris* (*Days of Wrath*, as the title is strangely rendered in Haakon Chevalier's translation of the novel), "virile fraternity goes . . . deep into the blood itself, into the hidden areas of the heart where torture and death are crouched and waiting." And it is on the fact of this power of the human communion to enliven the bloodstream of the heart and to fend off, at least in some degree, the powers of darkness—it is on this that Malraux's principal fictions are wanting to insist.

Though I associate myself with that minority of readers who think of Malraux's great book of 1937, *Man's Hope*, as his most impressive achievement in fiction, the general consensus does, of course, support the view that it is *Man's Fate* (1933) which is his masterpiece. But, however it may finally be ranked in relation to his other fictions, *Man's Fate* is unquestionably a work whose brilliance of organization and development must place it amongst the central texts of our century in the literature of the novel. And it is a book so capacious in the human material it includes as to be far richer in its complications and interlinkages than anything Malraux had previously done. Its narrative (like that of *The Conquerors*) is plotted against the background of the Chinese Revolution of the twenties, though now the scene is not Canton but Shanghai, which, in the winter of 1927, was where the increasing tensions within the Kuomintang (between Chiang Kai-shek's Nationalists and the Communist left-wing) were being most severely felt. Over the previous year the insurgents had captured not only Canton but also the industrial center of Hankow, and, as Chiang moved steadily northward, he determined that Shanghai must not be allowed, as Hankow had been, to fall under the sway of his unreliable Communist allies, whose intention he knew to be that of finally delivering him over to the Kremlin: so, in order to settle the issue, he shifted his course somewhat eastward and moved into the neighborhood of the city in February 1927, remaining in its outer precincts, however, until the Communists in late March mounted a successful *coup* against the local "warlord"—and then, early in the following month, he suddenly bore down upon them with a dispatch and ferocity so remorseless that they were utterly demoralized, and, before they could recover from the confusion, the city was in his hands—and the Communist insurrectionaries were being swiftly liquidated, with a singularly reckless cruelty.

Now it is on these events that Malraux's novel forms a kind of gloss, though they provide only the *mise en scène* in relation to which the novel conducts its principal inquiry, and this focuses not on the politics of the Chinese Revolution but on certain fictive personages whom Malraux involves in that struggle and on the various possibilities for reckoning with man's ultimate solitude that these figures exemplify. It is a large cast of characters that Malraux arranges, and all are *isolés*. The young revolutionist, Ch'en, though he has entered the world of terrorism and murder, keeps the searing consciousness of sin imparted to him as a boy by the Lutheran pastor under whose tutelage his conscience was deeply formed; and his inveterate sense of his own unlovableness so little prepares him in turn to offer love to others that he does at last become one for whom the act of murder itself affords the quintessential erotic experience. His companion in subversion, the half-caste Kyo, had supposed that at least in marriage there was some deliverance from one's isolation, but, when May confesses a casual infidelity, he suddenly realizes how tenuous is his relation even to his wife. And his father, the learned and imperturbable old contemplative Gisors, has long since given up any great expectations in regard to the human community: he finds his anodyne in the placid indifference induced by his opium, and his one bond with the world of men is his love for Kyo, who occasionally prompts in his father the sense of having ceased to feel that he does not even know his son. Or, again, there is the brutal French tycoon Ferral, who dwells in a wilderness of his own contriving: he is a frenzied sensualist of power who conceives all persons whom he encounters to be nothing more than mechanisms awaiting his manipulation—and most especially is this the case in his relations with women: yet, despite his sexual profligacy, "in reality," as we are told, "he never went to bed with anyone but himself." Nor is he very different from König, Chiang Kai-shek's chief of police, who is a man deformed by the humiliating memory of a time long ago in Russia when, under the stress of torture, he wept before his Bolshevik inquisitors—and his twistedness now expresses itself in a cruelty toward his own prisoners as obdurate as that before which he himself once quailed. And the seedy expatriate, the Baron de Clappique, who "feels a need to live inadequately," is so captive to his "mythomania" that he has very nearly slipped out of the world altogether, and he comes alive only by the roulette wheel or over a bottle of whisky. All these, and more—Katow, Hemmelrich, Kama—are people suffering deep, secret hurts that hopelessly yearn for a sympathy which they are not, however, themselves prepared in turn readily to offer others, for they are all islanders unschooled in the disciplines of brotherhood. Yet it is the purpose of the novel that some should be brought to the point of discovering—or at least of exemplifying—the grace and healing that are in "fraternity."

The tableau with which the narrative opens is, of course, one of the most memorable scenes in modern fiction. At a little after midnight, on the twenty-first of March, 1927, Ch'en stands silently in a Shanghai hotel room by the bedside of a sleeping man, with his eyes riveted on the dormant and utterly vulnerable body. And, as the muffled sound of traffic in the streets below drifts up through the open window, he wonders if he should try to raise the mosquito-netting that surrounds the bed or if he should simply plunge his dagger through the netting and into the exposed, fleshy breast of the half-naked slumberer who lies on his back. With great deliberateness he selects the precise angle from which the attack is to be made, and, at last, he strikes through the gauze, at arm's length, and "with a blow that would have split a plank." There is a moment in which, as he clings to the weapon, "a current of unbearable anguish" flows from the dying man through the dagger and into the very depth of the assassin's chest. But, in the next moment, the lifeless body gently sags sideways and downward. Then, after grabbing the papers that will enable his fellow revolutionists to lay hold of a shipload of arms, Ch'en leaves, locks the room, walks to the floor below, takes there an elevator to the hotel lobby, and moves out into the stir of a crowded thoroughfare where he hails a taxi.

By the next morning the campaign of the insurrectionists is launched: they, "elated and wary," are in command of the central posts of the local police: their troops appear to have the streets under control, and, thinking that they have only to take over an armored train, they begin to smell the odor of victory—which, as it seems, will be guaranteed by the entry into the city of Chiang Kai-shek's forces. But, given the suspiciousness that Chiang harbors toward the Comintern, they count on too much. For, once he is assured of support from European financial interests fearful of the area's being proletarianized, he feels himself able to chart a course of breaking loose from what he considers to be the potential treachery of his Marxist allies. And no sooner do they discover this shift in his designs than they begin desperately to seek support from the Third International's phalanx in Hankow, but there it is deemed unpropitious to venture at the moment any outright confrontation with Chiang. So Kyo and Ch'en and their comrades are left on their own, and ultimately at the mercy of the Nationalists which proves to be no mercy at all, for, once Chiang's men move into the city, the Shanghai rebels are tracked down with a terrible relentlessness —and their last state, indeed, is one of violent martyrdom.

It would seem, then, that Katow and Pei and Ch'en and Kyo and their various confederates do in the end taste the gall of a defeat quite as decisive as that suffered, say, by a Garine (in *The Conquerors*) or a Perken (in *The Royal Way*). Indeed, some of Malraux's interpreters, by way of such a comparison, have said in effect that *Man's Fate* does in truth line itself up essentially behind the sort of dark gravity being expressed in his earlier books: its ashes of frustration and failure are declared to signify most principally the absolute closures of possibility that comprise the human universe once it falls under the sign of *l'Absurde*. And, given the radically "tragic" destiny which it conceives to be man's portion in a godless world, there is no denying the fact that there is much in the novel that supports the kind of judgment rendered in Gabriel Marcel's early review in *L'Europe Nouvelle* (no. 799, 3 June 1933), that its "metaphysical pessimism . . . makes Schopenhauer look like [so much] milk-and-water." Yet the crucial role played in Malraux's design by two of his most focal personages, Kyo and Katow, ought to suggest that no finally adequate measure of his moral calculus here may be taken in these terms alone.

Kyo, to be sure—like Garine and Perken—"had chosen action, in a grave and premeditated way, as others choose a military career, or the sea." Yet he does not aim simply at *le combat décisif* whereby, through some act of sheer self-assertiveness, his scar may be left on the map of history. He is one in whom "the heroic sense" is powerfully active, but his restlessness commits him ultimately to something more serious than mere nihilist adventure, for his great purpose is that of giving to coolies and factory workers and disinherited peasants a sense of the ineradicable dignity that belongs to them by virtue of their manhood. "A half-breed, an outcast, despised by the white men and even more by the white women, Kyo . . . had sought and had found his own kind. 'There is no possible dignity, no real life for a man who works twelve hours a day without knowing why he works.'" And his election of a Marxist program has been prompted by his desire to find an effective political stratagem for honoring the sacrament of the brother: he wants to dedicate all his energies to the preparation of an order of life in which the master-slave relationship will have no place at all and in which the absurd humiliation of men by other men will be brought to an end. Nor is he prostrated with any sort of dispirited cynicism or heartache by the collapse of his revolt. He is thrown by Chiang's lieutenants into a makeshift prison that is filled with the stench of a slaughterhouse, and here he is beaten and tortured. He knows that the final agony reserved for him and his comrades by their captors is that of being thrown alive into the boiler of a locomotive, and he is not untouched by "the nauseating humiliation" that men feel when shorn of all power to resist brutality and maleficence. Yet, in the moment before he crushes between his teeth the pellet of cyanide that he has kept in his belt buckle for the last emergency, a strange peace settles down upon him, as it occurs to him to think that

> . . . everywhere where men labor in pain, in absurdity, in humiliation, they were thinking of condemned men like these, thinking as believers would pray; and, in the city, they were beginning to love these dying men as they would the already dead. In all of that which this last night overlay on the earth, this place of agony was no doubt the most weighted with virile love. He could wail with this crowd of prostrate men, join this sacrificed suffering even in its murmur of complaint. . . . He had fought for what in his time was charged with the deepest meaning and the greatest hope; he was dying among those with whom he would have wanted to live. . . . It is easy to die when one does not die alone.

True, the disappointment brought by his learning of his wife's infidelity had borne in upon him a deeply painful reminder of how inescapable is a man's fundamental solitude in even the most intimate relations of life. Yet, ontologically absolute as our human separateness appears to be, he has also discovered the opposite though equally absolute fact, that a great kind of transcendence of our solitude is possible in that rich fellowship which arises when men put aside all the vanities of self-preoccupation for the sake of a common endeavor in behalf of the oppressed and the downtrodden, the insulted and the injured—and he finds that, for this, it is not unbearably difficult to die.

Then there is one other figure whose way of facing these last hours reveals how surely Malraux's book of 1933 is pressing toward a vision of Exchange and Substitution as the true fundament of human life. For, along with Kyo in that fearful prison improvised by Chiang's men for the detention of the captured insurrectionists, there is the Russian Katow, who has been one of the chief organizers of the *coup* but whom we see little of throughout most of the action: yet it is he who is at the center of Malraux's great climactic scene and who is perhaps the novel's most exemplary embodiment of *fraternité virile*. Amidst their comrades' whispers of pain, he had lain beside Kyo in the large hall of their incarceration and, with a "brotherly quavering," had tenderly caressed the dying man in the final moments, as the cyanide was having its effect. And, after the last breath is convulsively wrenched from Kyo's anguished body, he feels that odd "sense of repose" he has previously known "in the worst moments of his life." But this strange languor is soon interrupted by the sound of the distant locomotive whistle which, as it reaches the hall, signals that another of their number has been thrown into the boiler. With this reminder of the frightful progress being made in their destruction, two young Chinese who are lying beside Katow begin to sob with panic, and one stutteringly cries out to him: "To be burned alive. The eyes, too, the eyes . . . each finger, and the stomach, the stomach. . . ." Whereupon the Russian, seized with pity for these terror-stricken boys and united to them by "that absolute friendship . . . which death alone gives," takes the pellet of cyanide he has been saving for himself, breaks it in two, and offers each a piece. Their bodies are soon stiffening, and, when a Kuomintang officer comes to summon him to his execution, he, "with uneven steps, hindered by his wounds," walks heavily toward a fiery extinction, as all those who remain in the hall follow "the rhythm of his walk, with love. . . ." It is one of the transcendent, and most deeply moving, moments of modern fiction—which says that the principle that unlocks and redeems the human mystery is that of Deputyship and Sacrifice.

The book immediately brought Malraux an immense acclaim and a new celebrity on the international scene. It won the Goncourt Prize in 1933, retaining even today the distinction of being one of the few genuinely important works to have been given this award since it was offered to Proust in 1919. And, as it were, overnight, this gifted young man found himself elected to the difficult role of Witness and Spokesman for the Leftist conscience. He was widely thought to be, if not a member of the Party, at least a sort of quasi Communist; and certainly for a time he was regularly to be found where, bearing such an allegiance, he might have been expected to be—at the First Congress of Soviet Writers in Moscow, in the Association of Revolutionary Writers and Artists, in Berlin with Gide to plead before Joseph Goebbels for the life of the Bulgarian Communist Giorgy Dimitrov, and on platforms all over the world arranged by Leftist coalitions. But the stricter sectarians in Marxist circles were never satisfied with Malraux's orthodoxy, conceiving it to be seriously flawed by "deviationist" tendencies in the direction of Trotskyism and by a lyrical individualism that, from their standpoint, appeared to represent merely an unreliable kind of obscurantism. And they, in their estimate, were far more right than journalists and literary intellectuals specializing in *Tendenz* who were often inclined in the 1930s simply to associate him in a loose sort of way with the Communist movement. For, amidst the alarming new emergencies precipitated by Hitler's resolve to make the Germans the *Herrenvolk* of Europe and the world, he would seem indeed to have felt that the great opposition of the period was between the values of liberal democracy and the atavistic demonry of Fascism. And it was in the ugly, threatening monomania of Caesarist autocracy that he found the great challenge of the time.

So it is not surprising that the scene of his book of 1935 is Hitler's Germany. *Days of Wrath* (whose French title—*Le*

Temps du mépris—would be perhaps more appropriately translated as *The Age of Contempt*), though conventionally spoken of as a novel, is in fact a long *nouvelle*. And the stark, bare simplicity of its recital ought to suggest how far off the mark are those who take it to have been calculated to be a piece of anti-Nazi propaganda, for, had this been Malraux's intention, he would surely have been at pains, as he hints in his Preface, to produce a heavily detailed account of the Nazi system in the idioms of a naturalistically ordered fiction. Instead, however, apart from his central character, the persons and places entering into the narrative are rendered in only the shadowiest terms, and the fable very clearly wants to put before us nothing other than one man reckoning with what Malraux would call his *destin*.

The protagonist is one Kassner, a writer, who has been playing a key role in the Communist underground in Germany. On a certain day he is arrested and submitted to interrogation by officers of the Gestapo. He is, of course, careful to be evasive and misleading, and, since the old photograph of him carried in the Gestapo files is too faded to permit his interrogators to establish beyond question his identity, he is imprisoned in a stone cell where he is beaten and tortured and then left simply to disintegrate under the pressures of solitary confinement. And the psychic stress of his ordeal, as it begins to express itself in wild nightmare and fantasy, is what chiefly frightens Kassner, for his great fear is that of so losing self-control as in some way to betray his confederates. He seeks desperately, but unavailingly, to order and stabilize the workings of his mind, and, just as he is beginning to slip into utter confusion, he is rescued from the brink of madness by the sound of another prisoner in a neighboring cell tapping out what appears to be a kind of code—five knocks, two, twenty-six; then a pause, followed by nine and then ten; and still other combinations are heard, again and again and again. At first these taps are only a hopeless jumble. But, in one of the great efforts of his life, he tries to summon up every last resource of patience and concentration at his command, as he undertakes to decipher the code. And, after trying countless hypotheses over a long stretch of time, he is at last shaken with a very nearly overpowering joy as he begins to break the cryptograph and to discover that the message being tapped out on the wall by this unknown fellow prisoner is "Comrade, take courage. . . ." Just at this point, however, the tapping ceases, and, from the same direction whence travel the knocks, there comes the sound of a door being slammed and then a series of heavy, muffled thuds—which he takes to be a sure sign that the guards have entered the cell and are brutally assaulting his unseen mate. Yet so profoundly enheartened is he by the words that have been tapped out to him on those prison walls that, his reason now restored, he begins to compose in his mind a long message of his own to those others of his comrades who may be incarcerated with him in the darkness of this prison.

Then, on the ninth day, as if the event had been arranged by the author of *Der Prozess*, his jailers suddenly release him, some other prisoner, under the stress no doubt of torture, having "confessed" that *he* is Kassner. He is taken to the nearest frontier, and there he is met by one—identified only as "the pilot"—who, as it would seem, has been commissioned to fly him over the Bohemian mountain range into Prague. It is a night of hail storms and fog, and the small single-engine plane, with its controls soon heavily iced over, crazily dips and swirls through the air, and, for a time, they seem bound to be flung down into the Carpathians by the scudding winds. In a desperate maneuver, the pilot shuts off his motor, and, by letting the plane simply drop, manages by the sheer weight of the fall to pierce through the storm and then to regain control. At last, the lights of Prague are seen shining on the horizon. And, after entering the city, Kassner makes his way on to his apartment where he is reunited with his wife Anna and their child.

Malraux's Preface says: "The world of a work like this, the world of tragedy, is always the ancient one: the man, the mob, the elements, the woman, destiny. It reduces itself to two characters, the hero and his sense of life. . . ." And, as he goes on to speak of Aeschylus and Corneille, one may well feel that he is by way of inserting this text into a range of literature comparison with which can only embarrass it, that so slender a tale as this simply cannot bear the kind of freight carried by the concept of tragedy. Nor would he himself seem now inclined to accord anything like the sort of importance to the book that the heavy sententiousness of his Preface was implicitly claiming forty years ago: indeed, his exclusion of it altogether in 1947 from the *Pléiade* collected edition of his novels suggests that he had truly meant what he said two years earlier to Roger Stéphane when, in speaking of the book, he declared: "It's a dud."[23] But we are often disposed to be excessively severe in appraising the work of our youth, and *Days of Wrath* deserves not to be simply dismissed as a fizzle but to be regarded as (in Professor Frohock's phrase) "another dry run, a trying out,"[24] of what was beginning to be Malraux's great theme—namely, the idea of *fraternité* as the essential adhesive of the human City.

It is true, of course, that the book is quite without the richness of psychological interest and episodic structure that belongs to *Man's Fate* and that we customarily expect a work of narrative fiction to entail. What is chiefly to the fore is nothing other than a bare prison cell, and into this black dungeon Malraux puts one whom, being stripped of all supports and defenses, he expects us to regard as an example of what *The Walnut Trees of Altenburg* calls "fundamental man." Moreover, he is proposing (as in *Man's Fate*) something like Pascal's suggestion of long ago (in the LXXIInd Fragment of the *Pensées*), that the appropriate image for the habitancy of "fundamental man" is that of a prison—where, alone and unassisted, he must reckon with the encumbrances of his finitude and face into the ultimate exigencies of suffering and death. Yet even in this extremity, Malraux wants to say, man is not utterly secluded and forsaken, for we are members one of another—and, though Kassner tries to stave madness off by rehearsing musical motifs of Bach and Beethoven, he is finally saved by some unknown comrade's tapping out on the wall of his own cell a message of courage, as he is also saved by still another who (for whatever reason) con-

23. Roger Stéphane, *Fin d'une jeunesse* (Paris: La Table Ronde, 1954), p. 51.
24. W. M. Frohock, *André Malraux and the Tragic Imagination* (Stanford: Stanford University Press, 1952), p. 94.

sents to say that *he* is Kassner—and, at the end, when all the commercial lines have grounded their planes because of the fiercely inclement weather, there is "the pilot" who, commissioned presumably by his comrades in the Underground, consents to brave the murderous airs and to fly him over the Carpathian mountain range into Prague. Which is to say that, in those perilous regions of life "where torture and death are crouched and waiting," it is fraternity, it is our mutual support and comfort of one another, that offer us our surest stay and succor.

But this great theme—of Deputyship and Sacrifice as the enabling principle of the human world—though it had begun to gather force in the meditation that underlay (very tentatively) *The Royal Way* and (more emphatically) *Man's Fate* and *Days of Wrath*, needed for its fullest exposition a larger, more complexly constituted theatre than could be afforded by the stripped down stage arranged by the book of 1935. It was such an arena, however, onto which Malraux was shortly to be propelled by the force of events, for, a few months after *Days of Wrath*—or *Le Temps du mépris*—was published in Paris by Gallimard, he was beckoned on to Spain, where the outbreak of civil war in that anxious summer of 1936 was to focalize for so many of his generation the issues of justice and freedom in a time when, as it seemed, the future of Europe (as of liberal democracy) was being called into question by the advance of Fascism. Franco's forces appeared at once to symbolize that advance and the possibility, at least in one corner of the world, of its being effectively resisted: so Malraux, along with countless others amongst the most gifted younger artists and intellectuals of the period, volunteered for service in the Loyalist cause. The Republicans did not, of course, finally prevail, but the experience of many of their English and European and American partisans did profoundly enrich the literature of modern testimony against tyranny—and, in this canon, *Man's Hope* (1937), the novel that resulted from Malraux's own time in Spain, is the great predominating masterpiece.

Despite the astonishing virtuosity with which its vast quantity of incident is arrayed and despite the lyrical eloquence with which the anguish of a particular moment of modern history is wrought into a metaphor of what is ultimately poignant in the human mystery, *Man's Hope* has somehow yet strangely failed to win an approbation commensurate with its actual weight and brilliance. It has consistently claimed the ardent admiration of a numerous company, and Henry de Montherlant's early acclamation of it as the book which above most others of its time "one would most like to have lived and written"[25] doubtless approximates the judgment that many others would be prepared to render; but, just as consistently, it has been caviled at in terms something like those either of R. W. B. Lewis, who speaks of it as "a showy and ultimately rather tiresome performance,"[26] or of W. M. Frohock, who considers it to be in part an anti-Fascist tract of the 1930s which "will survive more by its value as a document than as a piece of literature."[27]

The disappointment with the book which its detractors have expressed may well have been prompted in large measure by its refusal to fulfill some of the conventional expectations of prose fiction. Normally, of course, the novel is counted on to proffer a kind of direct, undogmatic reading of reality in the terms of "and then, and then, and then." And though the sequentiality of the narrative is expected to flow uninterruptedly, as if of its own accord, it is also expected that the anecdote will be carefully plotted, so that—by way of reversals and climaxes and denouements—it will gradually develop from its beginning through its middle to its end. The common assumption is that a novel will carry a large budget of events and will take its personages through many interesting vicissitudes and that, unless it is bent on becoming some kind of parable or apologue, it will shape its characters and episodes into a coherent and continuous *story*, in the manner of *Eugénie Grandet* or *The Wings of the Dove* or *Buddenbrooks* or *Women in Love*. But it was precisely

25. Henry de Montherlant, *L'Équinoxe de septembre* (Paris: Bernard Grasset, 1938), p. 91.
26. R. W. B. Lewis, "Introduction," in *Malraux: A Collection of Critical Essays,* ed. R. W. B. Lewis (Englewood Cliffs, N.J.: Prentice-Hall, 1964), p. 9.
27. W. M. Frohock, *André Malraux and the Tragic Imagination* (Stanford, Calif.: Stanford University Press, 1952), p. 125.

his having aimed at so panoramic a view of the Spanish tragedy as he managed indeed to achieve that committed Malraux
to a different procedure. Convinced as he was that the crisis in
Spain was but an omen of even larger and graver difficulties
awaiting the entire Western world, he wanted to deal with it *in
extenso* and from every possible angle—which meant that he
had to reckon not only with the Fascist insurgency but also with
the immense ideological diversification of the Republican movement, embracing as it did at once militant Communists, liberal
Anarchists, aroused trade-unionists, Catholic idealists, and a
variety of international adventurers. Moreover, not only did he
feel obliged to make room for a great populousness in his cast:
he also wanted to move freely back and forth across the entire
Spanish landscape—from Toledo to Madrid, from Málaga to
Barcelona, from the Jarama Valley to the Teruel mountains—
and thus to give us as wide a view as possible of all the major
fronts of the war, as it developed in the period scanned by the
novel, from the summer of 1936 to the late winter of 1937. So it
was natural that the cinematic method of *The Conquerors*
should here be very considerably extended and that he should
employ as his chief narrative stratagem a technique of *montage*
whereby snapshots of actions occurring in various locales might
be juxtaposed against each other and brief scenes might be so
"mounted" as to facilitate a swift movement from the large
panorama to the greatly intensified view of men and events at
close quarters. His transitions—from close-ups to mid-shots and
long-shots—are rapid, and the speed with which he "cuts" from
one scene to another hurtles us along through the action at so
great a pace that, if one fails to notice how surely and steadily
he is developing his primary themes, the whole performance
may then seem, indeed, to be merely a "showy" sort of stunt
unmarked by the triumphant integrity of such a book as *Man's
Fate*.

But that the novel, on any level at all, should be conceived to
be an essay in "Agit-Prop" is an utter amazement. True, *Man's
Hope* was written by one profoundly *engagé*, and Malraux was
of a quite simple mind regarding the ultimate righteousness of
the Republican cause; but the novel's political partisanship in

relation to the Civil War in Spain is at very nearly every point subordinated to its more fundamental concern, for what it wants most principally to do is to explore the essentially tragic nature of the political life.

Malraux's best readers have not failed to remark the heraldic rank that the manifest logic of *Man's Hope* does in effect accord the superscription heading the first section of its IInd Part, for, in the insistency with which its import resonates throughout the entire book, this phrase—*Être et faire* ("To Be and to Do")— does, indeed, consolidate the central issue.

Stuart Gilbert and Alastair Macdonald, in producing their English version of the novel, chose, quite unaccountably, to render the title of Part I—*L'Illusion lyrique*—as "Careless Rapture," and it was a foolish stroke that needlessly darkened Malraux's meaning. For the phrase wants nothing but a literal English translation, since it makes reference to the buoyantly "lyrical illusion" that took hold of Spanish liberals when, after the Franquist rebellion in July 1936, it seemed that at last an occasion had come when the inequities and humiliations that for centuries had belonged to the established order could be redressed. In the tableau arranged by *Man's Hope*, it is those liberal Republicans made up of Anarchists and "semi-Christians" and Catholic anti-clericals—such men as Hernandez and Puig, Ximénès and the Négus, Barca and Guernico—who are most moved by this apocalyptic presentiment of a new world in which swords will be beaten into plowshares, in which justice will roll down as waters, and righteousness as a mighty stream. These are the people, "the men of fraternity," who want to serve what the old art historian Alvear speaks of as "the human element; the quality of man." They hope, indeed, to create a new "People" dedicated to the inviolability of the person, but their sense of honor, their lust for nobility, will not allow them to permit expediency to justify any suspension, however provisional, of their chivalric code. Their dedication to the human future requires them to take up arms against their Fascist foe, but they are not so much men of the future as to be prepared, for the sake of eventual victory, to endorse any system or program of action that would require them *now* to betray their commitment

la sainteté de la présence humaine. For they are striking out
or a kind of richness and freedom of personal life that the old
rder denied: they want to extend the range of human possi-
ility: they want more fully to *be* men, and their consecration to
quality" persuades them that to take on the characteristics of
ie enemy, even if only as a temporary expedient, is to settle for
mode of death. So Hernandez, in the midst of the assault on
ie Alcazar at Toledo, consents to forward a letter from Mos-
ardo, the besieged commandant of the fortress, to his wife—for
ie sake of nothing other, as he says, than *générosité*; and, when
ebuked for his action by a comrade, he says simply: "What's
ie point of the revolution if it isn't to make men better?"

But, then, in the dialectic of the novel the men who are com-
itted to the art of "being"—those who want, as the Négus says,
:o live as life ought to be lived, here and now, or die"—are
anged over against the men who are interested in the craft of
loing." For these latter, for the "Organization Men" (who are,
 ideology, Communists)—for such stern combatants as Vargas
nd Golovkin and Pradas and Manuel—the apocalyptic moment
 which a new dawn is descried is but the first, inchoate stage
 a revolutionary process that requires to be skillfully and dis-
assionately ordered and administered; and they consider the
reat necessity of the hour to be that of transforming lyrical
aternity into an effective army. Early on in the novel, as the
attle at the Plaza de Cataluña in Barcelona is getting under
ay, it is said of the Anarchist Puig, as the men under his com-
and await his orders, that "all that lay deepest in his heart
orbade him to give orders." Yet there can be no army without
 chain of command. True, however just certain wars may be,
e are reminded by the head of the Loyalists' Intelligence Serv-
e that "there's no such thing as a just army—just as "there's no
ich thing as a just party." But Garcia wants also to insist that,
 this, the field of military life is by no means unique, for, as he
ys to the Italian Scali, "all forms of action are manichean, be-
use all action pays a tribute to the devil." By which he means
iat the great endeavors needing to be undertaken amongst men
an never be initiated and sustained merely by moral suasion,
iat there must always be ordinances that expediently establish

hierarchical imparities and lines of authority; and thus the lyri
cal fraternity out of which a populist insurgency is born can
become something consequential only insofar as it finally accede
to methods that do in large measure contravene the kind o
happy, impassioned communion of equals that provided the
whole original momentum. So, as Garcia says to Magnin, the
chief of the International Air Force, "Our humble task, Monsieu
Magnin, is to *organize* the apocalypse."

Far from having as its primary aim, then, any propagandisti
espousal of the Loyalist cause, the novel, as it moves about the
Spanish countryside and records the turbulence of the conflic
engulfing Toledo and Barcelona and Madrid, is most centrally
committed to a search for some way of resolving the bitter duali
ties contained within this troublesome dilemma of *être et faire*
Denis Boak, in his excellent book on Malraux, contends tha
at last "the main lesson" of *Man's Hope* is "that *être* is les
important than *faire*, that victory will be on the side, not of the
more just, but of the most efficient."[28] The neatness of hi
account, however, makes Malraux's moral calculus much tidie
than in fact it is, for what is most striking about the novel's de
sign is that it releases none of its major personages, not ever
its most hardheaded realists, from the exactions of its *embarra
du choix.*

The young Communist, Manuel, for example, feels nothing
but exasperation as he confronts the loftiness of those romantic
amongst the men under his command who, after the first sigh
of enemy casualties, are prepared to say, "But, after all, those
chaps haven't done us any harm." He knows that "to make
war successfully you must riddle . . . living flesh with fragments
of steel," and he is determined to *lead*, to forge his company
into a disciplined, reliable fighting force. But he is not an unre
flective man: though by profession a cinema sound-engineer, he
is a technician not without a considerable humanistic culture
and, though he does thoroughly master the lesson taught him by
Ximénès, that an officer must never court the approval and the
affection of his men, he still wants, nevertheless, to be loved

28. Denis Boak, *André Malraux* (London: Oxford University Press, 1968)
p. 111.

"it struck him that to make oneself loved without courting popularity is one of the finest careers a man can hope for." Yet there comes a time when, though he has proven himself a superbly effective officer, he realizes that, as he says, ". . . every step I've taken towards greater efficiency, towards becoming a better officer, has estranged me more and more from my fellow-men. Every day I'm getting a little less human." And he is not quite able to reconcile himself to what is by way of being lost. Nor can he suppress the anguish that springs up on that rainy night on the Madrid front when two court-martialed soldiers in his own brigade, having been sentenced to death for desertion, beseech him for their deliverance. He had himself ordered the tribunal, and yet, the verdict having now been rendered, as he looks down at the poor devils groveling at his feet, he is filled with distress. One of the suppliants (who looks "the very symbol of defeat—the eternal scapegoat, he who pays"), as he clings to Manuel's legs, with his breast heaving and his face dissolved in tears, rubs his cheeks frantically against his colonel's mud-smeared boots, crying: "They've no right to shoot us. . . . We're volunteers! You got to tell them. . . . They can't do it! . . . You got to tell them!" But the argument that touches Manuel to the quick is not a matter of the volunteer's having some right to exemption from the extreme penalty: it is, rather, simply the streaming face, the open mouth—"the everlasting visage of the man who pays." And, feeling that the sentence had been justly pronounced and that he is without any recourse in the matter of leniency, he is overborne by a sense of the tragic opposition between the claims of fraternity and those enjoined by the necessities of a great collective action.

Or, again, Garcia, the hearty and nonchalant anthropologist who is in charge of Loyalist intelligence operations, intends, despite his fatherly benignity, to be hard as nails about the fundamental requirements presented by the crisis. He takes it for granted that, as he says, ". . . a popular movement, or a revolution . . . can hold on to its victory only by methods directly opposed to those which gave it victory." For him it is axiomatic that "to make the revolution a way of living . . . [is to make it] a way of dying," that, unless the lyrical communion of Loyalist stalwarts is organized into an effective military and political force, it will perish: "We've got to . . . transform our apocalyptic vision into an army—or be exterminated." And he whose fastidiousness makes him burke at this necessity and say therefore in effect to the Nationalists and to the Loyalists, "A plague on both your houses"—such a man, in his outright abdication from responsibility, is, Garcia declares, simply "immoral"; and it is the example of Miguel de Unamuno which he has most immediately in mind. Yet, for all his own readiness to treat with what is inevitably "manichean" in revolutionary politics, Garcia is no more saved finally from an uneasy conscience by his roughcast kind of pragmatism than is Manuel. At a certain point, well on in the novel, as he looks one night at photographs of what Fascist bombs have done to Madrid and reflects on how in civil war cruelty invites cruelty as a rejoinder, he thinks of what the streets of the city were once like, "in the gay light of an April morning"—

> shop-windows, restaurants, women who were not to be slaughtered, and on the café terraces sugar-sticks dissolving like hoarfrost in glasses of water, beside cups of cinnamon-flavored chocolate. And now he sat alone in a deserted palace, confronting a polluted world, the very air of which was stifling. Whichever way this war ends, he mused, what sort of peace can possibly prevail after such bitter hatred? And what will the war make of me?

Then the crucial sentence recording his meditation says: "Moral problems! Yes, a man can never get away from them."

Indeed, neither Manuel nor Garcia nor Magnin nor Ximénès nor Guernico nor any of the major figures of the novel can be said simply to have collapsed the tension between "being" and "doing." All perhaps are more inclined towards the one or towards the other of the two alternatives, but, finally, none can absolutely elect the one and utterly abrogate the other: each is fated to live *within* this tension, and those valiants—like Puig and Hernandez—who die early and too soon may be considered (as Cecil Jenkins reminds us) to be, most essentially, the casualties of their own inability to straddle the antinomy between *être* and *faire*.[29]

29. See Cecil Jenkins, *André Malraux* (New York: Twayne, 1972), p. 99.

Yet the book is called *L'Espoir*. And the great concluding section, Part III, is called "L'Espoir." Which suggests that Malraux's intention was surely that of holding up some larger, more affirmative vision of human destiny than any predicated merely on our unalleviable entrapment within the contradictions of morality and revolutionary politics; and his great final task is that of suggesting what indeed it is that may be the ground of our ultimate hope for the human City.

As the novel moves toward its close, it appears that the confusions within the Loyalist ranks that led to the debacle at Toledo in September 1936 are being surmounted and that now, in the winter of 1937, Madrid will be successfully defended and possibly become the graveyard of the Nationalist movement. The rhapsodists of fraternity on the Republican side have perforce had to reckon with practical necessity and convert themselves into an effective fighting instrument. The force of events has made it impossible any longer for "being" and "doing" to be conceived as alternatives equally open and admissible: if the Fascist adversary is to be repulsed and the war is to be won, it is clear that the hazards of action simply may not be dodged, and thus, for the more sensitive men, the great question is no longer whether one shall undertake to "be" *or* to "do" but, rather, how it may be possible to develop a style of *faits* which is itself modulated and informed by the virtues of *être*.

At this late point in Malraux's chronicle, it is Magnin who is the decisive figure. Though he is himself a highly trained engineer, his hope has always been that the war might not be merely a technicians' war but a truly collective effort that would entail the shaping of a new People, and it is this lofty aspiration that has fed the extraordinary passion and energy with which he has devoted himself to the formation of the International Air Force. This Frenchman conceives himself to be in Spain to implement a great dream, of a commonwealth in which no man shall be humiliated and in which all shall have a chance at fulfillment. "I want each individual man," he says, "to have a life that isn't classified in terms of what he can exact from others." And he brought to Spain the conviction that, unless the war itself could be waged in a spirit consonant with the ultimate ends being sought, there could be no true victory in the end, whatever the outcome of the military engagement: higher values, in other words, than those of military efficiency were to be served by the machine of the Republican war effort itself. But, as Garcia had warned, he does himself discover in due course that he cannot keep his aviation corps up to the mark on the basis of mere fraternity, that only by organization and discipline can it be kept from becoming a fractious and demoralized rabble. Moreover, the battering suffered by the patched-up old crates which his men are flying does, in the course of time, result in such attrition for his beloved squadron that he has to regroup his planes and pilots, mingling them with those of the Spanish Air Force—where the rigorously sectarian spirit of the Communists has by this point made such inroads that, inevitably, for this generous and humane socialist that fine flush of buoyancy and ardor that had once been a part of the whole venture wears off, and he is left sad at heart. It seems indeed, as Garcia maintains, that "the age of parties is beginning."

But then there comes a great, uplifting moment—towards which, as it appears in retrospect, the entire action of the novel has been entrained—when Magnin is granted, along with ourselves, a vision of what it is that, beyond all the ambiguous relativities of the political order, deserves to command our trust and veneration. The bombing of a Fascist airfield on the Saragossa road has failed, because the planes which were to be destroyed are sheltered in an adjacent wood; and Garcia sends down one evening to Magnin on the Levant front a peasant who knows the area and who is confident that he can spot the safehold from the air. "You find me the Saragossa road," he says, "and I'll find you the field. Without any trouble at all." So Magnin decides to dispatch his planes the next morning at dawn. But since they will be setting out in darkness and since his own poorly equipped base is without groundlights, he must first travel about for several miles throughout the neighborhood to ask farmers here and there in the vicinity to drive their old cars and trucks to the field at that early morning hour, in order that, with their headlights, there may be sufficient illumination for the takeoff. And at the appointed time they appear, first one and then another, coming in their broken-down old vehicles from village after village. By half-past four eighteen machines have lurched into the area of the airstrip, some of the drivers having even brought hurricane lamps. And as these peasants stand stiffly about in the damp, predawn chill, they, utterly devoted to the Loyalist cause, ask, "Isn't there any other job we could do?" It is an immensely touching scene.

Then, at five o'clock, the planes take off for the Teruel front: there are only three—first, the plane being flown by Moros, then Pujol's, and then Magnin's. They are soon over the enemy lines and in sight of the Saragossa road. At first, Magnin's peasant guide is utterly disoriented and cannot "read" the landscape from the air; but he soon gets his bearings and points them on to the hidden field which is successfully demolished. In turning about, however, for the return flight the squadron is attacked by Fascist pursuit planes the fire from one of which strikes Pujol's old crate and sends it crashing down into the Teruel mountains, near the little village of Valdelinares.

Immediately after Magnin and Moros return to their landing field, Magnin undertakes to determine the exact location of the fallen plane and, after extensive inquiries, discovers that, high up on the slopes of the Sierra de Teruel, Pujol, having been able to walk from the wreck into the village of Valdelinares, has alerted the people there and that they have been attempting to turn up a physician for the injured flyers. He reaches Pujol by telephone and learns that only one of the airmen—the Arab, Saïdi—is dead. Then it is agreed that Pujol and the villagers out of straps and mattresses will try to improvise stretchers for the descent, as Magnin meanwhile will seek to get to the village of Linares, a little farther down in the Teruel range, and there organize rescue teams to meet the caravan. And from this point on Magnin is "in contact with the very soul of Spain." When he gets to Linares, he finds that the entire village is ready and eager for the ascent. He does not need so large a crew of attendants, but all insist on going, the old and the young, "keeping him stern and dignified company."

So they proceed up into the steep, snow-blanketed highlands, and, after a few difficult hours along their sheer, rocky, frozen path, they meet the stretchers coming down. Pujol and his copilot Langlois have escaped serious injury, but the others are fearfully hurt. Gardet's face is slashed open from ear to ear and he must use the butt of his revolver to support his broken jaw. The bombardier's leg is broken. Mireaux's sagging arm is very nearly ripped off, and his pain is so great that it has brought back into his face "the look of childhood." Scali carries an explosive bullet in his foot. And bringing up the rear of the procession is the body of Saïdi, the dead gunner, in a simple coffin onto the lid of which the people of Valdelinares have tied not a wreath but one of the twisted machine guns from the wreckage.

Now, the cortege spread out along the great wall of the mountain, the descent begins, moving slowly but steadily down the vast, rocky ravine towards the valley far below in which the little village of Linares is snugly nestled. And, as Magnin looks at "the solemn, primitive march" from atop the unsaddled mule which he teeteringly bestrides, it strikes him as having about it something as ageless and fundamental as the deep gorges into which they are plunging and the massive rocks that graze the lowering sky. The peasants bear the bloodstained men down the slopes with a clumsy yet competent gentleness, as the women, with "scarves on their heads and baskets on their arms," bustlingly move from one stretcher to another, desperately eager to perform whatever little service may in some slight degree alleviate the suffering but just as eager to try to conceal the depth of feeling that prompts their solicitude. From the bearers can occasionally be heard the quiet grunts that tell of physical effort, but they are always careful not in any way needlessly to jolt the stretchers. And the steady rhythm of the whole company's tread down the mountainside carries something like the "solemn beat . . . [of] a funeral drum." Yet in truth it is no death which haunts this craggy landscape, for the peasants' long procession has "more of the character of an austere triumphal progress than a relief party bringing home wounded men."

As they approach the village of Linares and the gradient eases the whole populace is gathered to watch the bearers pick their way carefully along, and over the entire crowd falls "a hush so profound . . . that the noise of the distant mountain-torrents [is] suddenly . . . audible," the silence being just merely broken by the quiet weeping of the women. The injured men (except Gardet, who is only barely alive) make an effort to smile at the villagers, and the hundreds of peasants, "determined [most especially when they catch sight of the coffin] to make some gesture," silently raise their clenched fists in a salute of homage and solidarity. Then the waiting ambulance hurries the flyers off across the misty countryside, and, amidst the light rain that has begun to fall, the massed villagers continue to stand "motionless with raised fists," as they peer into the distances at the vanishing carriage.

It is a pageant—the whole episode of the descent—whose beautiful gravity makes one of the most poignantly sublime scenes in the literature of the modern period, a drama indeed of which it could be said (as James Agee remarked of the rendering of it in the extraordinary film version of *L'Espoir* that Malraux produced with his friend Edward Corniglion-Molinier) that "Homer might know it . . . for the one work of our time which was wholly sympathetic to him."[30] And it is what Magnin finds here amongst these Spanish peasants, in the way of fidelity and gentleness and compassion, that seals in his heart a kind of guarantee that "the age of parties" shall not ultimately prevail and that, for all the provisional betrayals of the human communion that may be entailed in our various attempts to deal responsibly with the ambiguities of history, it is indeed the glory of *fraternité* which is the true norm and end of man's life on this earth. In short, the "hope" of which the novel wants finally to speak is one whose ground is given in Scali's word to old Alvear, that

". . . men who are joined together in . . . a common quest have, like men whom love unites, access to regions they could never reach left to themselves. And there's more nobility in the *ensemble* . . . than in almost any of the individuals composing it."

Now, as one views today Malraux's entire *oeuvre* in fiction, the great scene of the descent-from-the-mountain in *Man's Hope*

30. James Agee, *On Film* (New York: McDowell, Obolensky, 1958), p. 242.

does appear, penultimately, to look toward a similar scene in what one suspects to be, though it was written over thirty years ago, the last of his novels—namely, *Les Noyers de l'Altenburg* (*The Walnut Trees of Altenburg*). This book, first published in Lausanne (Éditions du Haut-Pays) in 1943, had in fact been written two years earlier. Immediately after the German invasion of Poland in September 1939, Malraux had volunteered for service in the French Army and joined a tank corps from which he was not separated until his unit was captured by German forces advancing across the plains of Flanders in mid-June of 1940. For his company internment followed, in a prisoner-of-war camp improvised by the Germans in the little cathedral town of Sens; and he was unable to contrive his escape until the following November, when he managed to break through the barbed wire and to get down to the south of France, where, not far from Monte Carlo, he settled in the town of Roquebrune and took a lease on a handsome villa. It was here that he was to remain until late in 1942, when he stealthily made his way into German-occupied Toulouse, from whence by the winter or early spring of the following year he had moved into the Corrèze, where, as "Colonel Berger," he took command of a small band of *maquisards*. And it was in Roquebrune—in the dark days of 1941, after the collapse of France—that *The Walnut Trees of Altenburg* was written. It was designed to be but the first part of a three-volume novel which he was intending to call *La Lutte avec l'ange* (*The Struggle with the Angel*), but, unfortunately, the manuscripts that had resulted from his initial labors on the remaining parts of this vast project fell into the hands of the Gestapo during the war years and were destroyed. Which led him in the Preface he prepared for the 1948 edition issued in Paris by Gallimard to suggest—when he was still apparently inclined to promise an eventual completion of the work—that, indeed, once *The Walnut Trees of Altenburg* found its place within the entire chronicle, it would "no doubt be radically changed"; and thus, as he said, in its present form it can "appeal only to the curiosity of bibliophiles." But today it is not thought likely that Malraux will ever resume this whole effort, and the fragment we have must therefore simply be taken on its own terms—which it is not at all difficult to do, since it has a very remarkable unity that does not seem to need any sort of extension by a larger pattern.

Indeed, *The Walnut Trees,* in the marvelously affecting poem it projects on the central themes of his lifelong meditation, stands now as a consummate instance of Malraux's art and as one of the great, though strangely not much read, books of our time. And one thinks of it, indeed, as being something like a poem. True, the poetry is not, as in so much of his earlier writing, an affair of the mercurial histrionism with which discrete scenes and images are flung into dramatic structures by a kind of cinematic parquetry, for in the book of 1941—despite the great gaps between its major parts—this mode of narration gives way to a more continuous, more consecutive, kind of chronicling. Here, the presence conveyed by the whole tone and ethos of the novel is that of a brooding *raisonneur* who aims (like Garcia in *Man's Hope*) at "converting as wide a range of experience as possible into conscious thought," who conceives *thinking well* to be the very definition of virtue; and it is the whole action represented by his search after the "fundamentality" of man which, in its austere yet lyrical purity, commands such a response as we accord large poems whose principal objective is *philosophia,* or wisdom.

The first of the novel's five main parts has as its setting an internment camp which in the spring of 1940 the invading German forces have arranged in the cathedral precincts in Chartres for their newly taken French prisoners; and the date is 21 June. The narrator is a young Alsatian named Berger, who, prior to his capture, had been serving in a French tank corps. And now, amidst the hundreds of shivering, bewildered prisoners who fill the vast nave of this great old Gothic church—as he notices in the flickering light how they hoard their little tins of food, how they busily scribble off letters to wives and sweethearts which they know their captors will never mail, as he remarks how each seeks to establish a certain little space as *his*— the pathos of this whole struggle to endure makes him feel that at last he is facing the real essence of that with which he, as a writer, has been seeking to reckon over many years: namely, the human mystery itself. Indeed, he is put in mind of his dead father, Vincent Berger, who often said that "It is not by any amount of scratching at the individual that one finally comes down to mankind." And since, in his place of incarceration, "writing is the only way to keep alive," he resolves to try to put in order his own experience of the world by attempting a reconstruction of his father's "'encounters with mankind'" (as they were spoken of in the mass of notes which he never had a chance to shape into the formal autobiography he was projecting):

> I was wounded on the 14th, taken prisoner on the 18th; his fate in the other war—and on the other side—was decided on June 14th, 1915. Twenty-five years ago, almost to the day. He was not much older than myself when he began to feel the impact of that human mystery which now obsesses me, and which makes me begin, perhaps, to understand him.

This brief prologue is then followed by the three central chapters of the novel each of which is devoted to a major episode in the life of the narrator's father. In the first segment of this trilogy Vincent Berger, a native of Alsace (then a part of the German Empire), is a junior professor at the University of Constantinople, where, in 1908, his first course of lectures is devoted to Nietzsche and "the philosophy of action." And since the German ambassador rightly suspects that, with him, action comes before philosophy, once he discovers how well informed Berger is about the Young Turk movement, he quickly offers him a post as director of the Embassy's propaganda efforts in Turkey. Nor is the young man slow to seize the appointment: "his need to get away from Europe, the lure of history, the fanatical desire to leave some scar on the face of the earth, the fascination of a project to which he had contributed not a few of the finer points"—all this prompts him to plunge with a great enthusiasm into the dark complexities of pre-1914 Balkan politics. The German envoy had only intended that his efforts should be calculated to guarantee, in the event of a European war, a Turkish alliance with Germany. But Vincent is soon mesmerized by Ottoman nationalism. He comes to be widely known as the *éminence grise* behind Enver Pasha and (in the manner of a T. E. Lawrence) undertakes to help him build a new empire that shall unite "all Turks throughout Central Asia from Adrianople to the Chinese oases on the Silk Trade Route." After many months of journeying across the steppes of Central Asia in an effort to galvanize the entire Islamic world, he discovers, however, that the old Turanism exists only as a figment of Enver Pasha's inflamed imagination, that the Moslem khans have no interest in any sort of pan-Ottomanism, and that in fact he is dealing with an irredeemably somnolent people for whom "life is a random chapter in the destiny of the universe," who are "sleep-walking among their ruins." So, after having spent six years in the East, he books passage at Karachi on a cargo vessel which takes him first to Port Said and from thence to Marseilles; and, five days after his return to his home in Reichbach, his father, the eccentric Dietrich Berger, commits suicide.

Vincent's next "encounter with man" occurs in the spring of 1914 at the old abbey of Altenburg in Alsace which his father's brother Walter has purchased for use as a conference center: here he annually gathers—as in fact Paul Desjardins did for many years at Pontigny—groups of distinguished European intellectuals for colloquies over which he presides as impresario and chief arbiter. He had at first chosen as the theme for his 1914 colloquy "The Eternal Elements of Art," but his unsettlement by his brother's death leads him finally to decide that the discussions shall be addressed to the question "Is there something given on which we can base the notion of man?" "In other words: under the beliefs, the myths, especially under the multiplicity of mental structures, is it possible to distinguish a permanent line or idea which retains its validity through history and on which the notion of man can be based?" And since Vincent's Turkish adventure has given him on the European scene the glamor of one who, indifferent to gain and to power, has been involved in clandestine missions and diplomatic cabals of high importance, his uncle has been particularly eager that he should be present.

The colloquy gathers a good deal of intensity as it proceeds, so much so that all the participants eventually feel themselves to be on trial. Yet the discussion can hardly be said to issue in any genuine resolution of the fundamental issue: instead, the various speakers simply deliver their arguments, each wanting, one feels, by the force of his own rhetoric to reduce the others to speechlessness, and, of these, it is the German ethnologist Möllberg who, even if he does not manage to frame any true unanimity, succeeds in being the most voluble and the most vociferous. Count Rabaud—whom it has "taken . . . thirty years to acquire the airs of a Mallarmé"—proposes that "the continuity of man" is in the keeping of the artist, since he has the power of so substantializing an Orestes or a Hamlet or an Ivan Karamazov as to enable us to enter into the destinies of those far removed from us in space and time. But Edmé Thirard denies that masterpieces offer any true disclosure of the nature of man: on the contrary, they only tell us something about that small minority of men who are capable of producing and appreciating them: no, says Thirard, it is not by the religion of culture that we shall be saved, and he maintains that it is compassion that affords us the deepest knowledge of man, of what the novel speaks of at one point as "the commonplace human mystery . . . [to be] come across . . . in hospitals, in maternity wards, and in the rooms of the dying." But he in turn is interrupted by the great commentator on the German Middle Ages, Stieglitz—and so on they go, "screeching" out at one another their various interjections, as Walter Berger occasionally intervenes with his little coughs which mean "No bickering." It is all, Vincent feels, "a dialogue with culture" in which an idea is "never born of a fact, but always of another idea." He does himself quietly suggest at one point that the really crucial consideration is to be found in the doggedness with which man constantly struggles with the great issues of fate and destiny and that perhaps the best answer, therefore, to the question of his true identity is one which says in effect that he is the creature who is forever engaged in an attempt at "humanization of the world." But this is a proposal that does not quite manage to carry the day.

Then at last the great Möllberg steps in, and, as notebooks are taken out, a new suspense is felt in the high, vaulted Romanesque room. He, with the imperturbable self-assurance of the *Kulturphilosoph* enchanted by his own opinions, lays it down that there simply is no such thing as "fundamental man," that this is nothing but a sentimental myth cherished by intellectuals. And he proceeds, in a manner very much reminiscent at once of Frobenius and of Spengler, to declare that there can be no more communication between cultures than there can be between a caterpillar and a butterfly, for each has its own coherence, its own system of belief, its own myths, its own sense of time. There are, for example, he says, certain Melanesian tribes that "have not discovered the connection between the sexual act and birth"; or, again, he cites certain societies in Australia and Alaska in which there is no system of exchange, as he also cites ancient Egyptian burial customs as betraying a conception of death utterly different from that belonging to modern European culture. And he asks, "Between the men we have just mentioned, and the Greek, or the Gothic man—or anybody else—and ourselves, what is there in common?" But, of course, his question is purely rhetorical, for his whole argument is to the effect that the human individual is little more than an epiphenomenon of the particular cultural matrix by which he has been formed and that, given the unbridgeable disjunctions between cultural systems, there is no ground on which it is possible to posit any conception of man *qua* man, of man *as such.* Thirard suggests that surely, for example, the dispossessed of one culture will be found in certain respects to resemble the dispossessed of another culture, to which Möllberg's reply is that, no, to be excluded from one's own culture is simply to "fade away"—into "oblivion." Then he points to some little Gothic sculptures in the room where they are gathered which are carved of walnut, and he says that these forms are not shaped from "fundamental walnut": no, they were simply hewn from logs of wood—and he proposes that the idea of "fundamental man" is just as chimerical as would be the idea of some "fundamental walnut" intermediate between these figurines.

At last the day's discussion is over, and, the colloquists now being free to go their separate ways until the dinner hour, Vincent wanders off at sunset into the orchards that, just beyond the Altenburg priory, crown the hills that roll down to the Rhine. He finds himself after a time standing by two magnificently venerable walnut trees whose great bulk frames the twi-lit contours of Strasbourg Cathedral in the distance. And as he looks at these "two sturdy, gnarled growths" the strength of whose boughs is dragged out of the very earth itself and as he thinks of how these massive columns of wood and leafage and fruit have *lasted*, he is suddenly granted a presentiment of the steadfastness and survivance and perenniality that are unde-niably a part of our world—and, in this moment, he knows two things: that before the statues and before the logs there were these trees, and that the idea of "the continuity of man," of "fundamental man," is not the absurdity Möllberg has declared it to be.

The third and final episode in Vincent's career which his son recounts is one that occurs on the twelfth day of June, 1915. The Great War is well under way, and he, as an officer in the German Intelligence Service, is on the Vistula front where his assignment is that of safguarding one Professor Hoffman, a chemist who has been brought into the Eastern sector to super-vise the handling of a new poisonous gas of his own invention which is to be used in an attack on the Russians. The professor, however cunning he may be in his laboratory, is a coldhearted, mindless fool with an inordinate zest for chemical warfare: he chatters endlessly about the respective merits of various gases, and, at the approach of the appointed hour for the attack, he chirps away ever so happily, like a madman, about how "per-fect" the conditions are. The infantrymen, however, as they await in their dugouts the signal for the beginning of their bombardment, talk as their kind have always talked: it is the coarse, hearty, demotic patois of plain men. One says that the Czar is a humbug, for, instead of marching at the head of his men, he remains safely in his palace at St. Petersburg. Another speaks boastfully of the "brain-work" required by his job as a die-stamper back at home. A miner salaciously describes how the workers in his pits wear only pants, even the women; and he is stirred at the thought of their naked torsos. Another voice speaks of a chap who had been on the Western front and who, on returning home for his furlough, discovered his wife's in-fidelity:

"It was night time, he knocked: no answer. And he knew his old woman was there all right! He went on knocking nearly all night. She didn't answer. She didn't want to. Then he understood. He went back to the squadron, and then he hung himself."

One young man is to be heard saying of his wife's photograph which he is exhibiting to his mates, "It wasn't for her looks I married her." And still another says: "Well, you know, my wife's not much to look at either." As he crouches with the professor in their observation-hole and listens in the "live darkness," Vincent feels that for the first time perhaps he is in touch with "the people of Germany"—or, as he thinks, with "just . . . men."

And then comes the great, decisive moment in which he discovers what "fundamental man" really is, or what he is capable of in the way of self-transcendence. The signal is given, the gas is released, and it floats over the tall, tufted grass and down the adjacent valley toward the Russian trenches. The men wait, and they wait, and they continue to wait, but, through their binoculars, they can descry no activity in the area of the enemy's advance positions: not the merest trace of anything is to be seen across the half-mile or so dividing their lines from the Russians', and they begin to wonder if perhaps some notice of the attack had been circulated and if, therefore, the trenches at which they are aiming have been vacated. The professor's nose is twitching, and he is panting with impatience, as he peers anxiously through his field glasses. Finally, they decide to move forward, and first one line and then another cautiously advances—but still no fire comes from the Russian artillery.

Meanwhile, Vincent and the other staff officers who are watching the advance through their binoculars wonder why it is that their men, after plunging into the Russian trenches, do not reappear. Then after an interval they can be seen emerging, but, instead of moving on towards the Russians' second lines, they are coming back in a great swarm and mysteriously carrying what from the distance of nearly a mile can be made out to be only white spots. The officers are utterly baffled by this queer spectacle, and Vincent, being no longer able to contain his curiosity, hops onto a horse and dashes forward. And, as he approaches the area over which the gas has passed, he begins to behold the unbelievable horror that has been wrought. Trees, flowers, grass—everything has been blackened and decomposed, or strangely petrified: the very earth itself is dead, its foul mud awakening "the same disgust that life feels for carrion." His horse is so terrified that it pitches him off and hysterically bolts into the woods. When he reaches the far side of the area, he begins to meet the troops limping through the awful foulness and wildly babbling out their dread and panic. And he discovers what those white spots are they had been seen from a distance to be carrying: they are the dying Russians, naked because when first assaulted by the gas they had torn off their uniforms. One of the German troops, as he lumbers past with a dead Russian on his shoulders, cries out: "No, man wasn't born to rot!" At every point on the terrain men are to be seen carrying other men, "their ranks broken and re-broken by the anthill confusion of their flight." As he watches "the assault of pity tumbling down towards the ambulances," Vincent suddenly knows that he, too, must find a body not yet dead and take it up on his back: he begins to mumble " 'Quickly, quickly,' not knowing what he . . . [means] . . . and no longer even aware that he . . . [is] walking," for he, like all the Germans in the field, is overborne with a frightful sense of the Spirit of Evil being in this place. He picks up a man writhing in the decomposed grass and, with "his whole body glued to this brother's body," begins to carry him away. But he soon realizes that the poor wretch is dead and lets him go. At last, however, having himself inhaled a large amount of the poisonous vapors, he collapses; and the final sentence of the chapter, in speaking simply of his complete loss of consciousness, conveys unmistakably the hint of his death being imminent.

As he had stumbled about through that infernal wood and gaped at his comrades retreating under the weight of their dying Russian foes, Vincent had vaguely wondered, "Was it pity?" But he had decided that, no, "it was something a good deal deeper, an impulse in which anguish and fraternity were inseparably mingled, an impulse that came from far back in the past"—an impulse indeed which, as it prompts us to bear the *other*'s burdens and to acknowledge the Coinherence of all life, is wrought into the very fiber of the human heart. And though Malraux's last recourse does not at all tend normally to be that of the Christian *mythos*, it would seem that, in designing the great climactic moment in *The Walnut Trees of Altenburg*, he could not resist a deeply felt urge to remind us that those disciplines of Substitution and Exchange and Sacrifice which are enjoined by the fact of our being "members one of another" have as their preeminent sign the sign of the Cross. For just before the gas attack begins, while Vincent and the men are waiting for the signal in the darkness of their dugouts, he suddenly notices that "On someone's chest, close to him, a ray of light was shining with the brilliance of an electric bulb, on the arms of a cross and the luminous bead of the Huguenot dove." Moreover, in the midst of the mutiny, as he passes a German infantryman struggling to carry on his shoulders a dying Russian out of "the sordid world of the liquefied forest," he notices that the two together outline in silhouette something like the Descent from the Cross. And it is such images which suggest that the "secret life" wherewith Vincent feels the whole terrible scene to be somehow quickened is none other than that strange solicitousness born of (as St. Paul speaks of it) a "godly sorrow"[31] which, as it takes hold of these rough combat troops, makes a kind of figure of what Charles Williams called "the demanded *caritas*"[32]—the *caritas*, that is, which was incarnate in the *Agnus Dei*.

The novel's epilogue returns us to the war-torn scene of Europe in the spring of 1940, though its action occurs somewhat earlier than the action of the prologue, for young Berger, Vincent's son, has not yet been captured and is still with his tank corps. The episode is largely devoted to a terrifying night that he and his crew spend in their tank, after it falls sideways into a ditch somewhere on the Flemish plains. Throughout most of

---

31. See 2 Corinthians 7:10—"For godly sorrow worketh repentance unto salvation, a repentance which bringeth no regret: but the sorrow of the world worketh death.."
32. Charles Williams, *He Came Down from Heaven*, p. 96.

the night they are expecting momentarily to be blasted by the German artillery, but they remain untouched, and, finally, the tracks of the tank begin to grip sufficiently for them to be able to steer their way out of their gutter and to move forward—by which time the Germans have departed. The next morning, when they reach the nearest village, they find it deserted: only an old peasant and his wife, too enfeebled to have fled, stay on. She says: "What else can we do? You, you're young; when you're old, there's nothing left but wear and tear." Then—slowly, pensively—she smiles at Berger and his mates, and he is filled with happiness, for the quiet composure with which she and her husband face the ultimate emergencies of life seems, unaccountably, to confirm the sense that their deliverance from the previous night's terror has brought, as he marvels at the sky and the sun and the few hens still strutting about the old peasants' barnyard—the sense that the gift of life and the gift of our own humanity are an extraordinary blessing. "I now know," Vincent's son says to himself, "the meaning of the ancient myths about the living snatched from the dead. I can scarcely remember what fear is like; what I carry within me is . . . a simple, sacred secret." But now, of course, we are aware that this "simple, sacred secret," given what he knows of his father's "encounters with man," is not merely an affair of his experience of the previous night ranged against this happy morning, that this precious knowledge he carries within himself is in large measure something inherited—namely, the knowledge *de père en fils* that there is an occasion for joy not only in the things and creatures of earth but also in the capacity of the human heart to be responsive to that on which the human City itself is founded, this being nothing other than the requirement of *caritas,* or, in Malraux's preferred designation of it, *fraternité.*

Many years ago Malraux suggested that the literary tradition of France may be thought of as having two major currents, the one descending from Pascal and Corneille and the other from Montaigne and Molière: the former, he said, represents an "effort . . . to make man participate in the privileged part of his being—or in that which surpasses him," whereas the latter seeks "to reduce to a minimum the part of comedy natural to the human state."[33]   And though the gnomic obscurity of the distinction being drawn here is not easily penetrable, one feels that his instinct about the nature of French tradition was surely right, as was also his declared sense of himself as belonging in the Pascalian line.   For the literature of France does in many ways ask to be thought of as centered about a great dialogue between those (Montaigne, Descartes, Molière, La Bruyère, Voltaire, Stendhal), on the one hand, who are devoted to the naked truth of common sense and who cultivate the virtues of reason and wit and lucidity and those (Pascal, Corneille, Bossuet, Lamartine, Vigny, Baudelaire), on the other hand, for whom the uses of this world are stale and unprofitable and who are distinguished by the spirit of anguish and *inquiétude* with which they conduct their inquiries into the human condition.   So centrally fixed in the history of their spirituality do the French consider this divide to be that the study of it is made, year in and year out, a principal element in the curriculum of the *lycée*; and Malraux does, indeed, deserve to be thought of as belonging on the side over which Pascal is the great presiding genius. He is, of course, quick to say, as he did recently to Guy Suarès, that, though Christianity has "a reality" for him that Buddhism or any other non-Western religion could never have, he is not in fact a believing Christian.[34]   And thus he is not an heir of the Pascal who meditates in the *Pensées* on "the Mystery of Jesus" and the miraculous "proofs" of the Christian faith; but he is very much an heir of the Pascal who explored those dark, unsettling regions of experience at which the wager of faith is directed. Which is to say that the Pascalian *problem*—of the strange disadvantage at which we are placed by the mutilations consequent upon our finitude, of the disproportion between man's frailty and the silent immensities of the universe—is Malraux's own most essential problem.   Like the brilliant son of Port-Royal, he, too, is obsessed by the world's absurdity, and, again and again, the idiom of his fiction is unmistakably Pascalian—as

33. An Interview with Malraux," in *Horizon,* vol. 12, no. 70 (October 1945), p. 242.

34. Guy Suarès, *Malraux: Past, Present, Future,* trans. Derek Coltman (Boston: Little, Brown and Co., 1975), p. 62.

when, for example, Vincent Berger reminds the colloquy at Altenburg "that we did not choose to be born. . . . That we did not choose our parents. That we can do nothing about the passage of time. That between each one of us and universal life there is a sort of . . . gulf."

Indeed, it is with the question of how this gulf, this *crevasse*, may be filled that Malraux has been wrestling for nearly fifty years. And the clues that most fully reveal the direction he has taken are to be found in the great crucial scenes of his fiction— in Katow's giving up his pellet of cyanide in *Man's Fate* to the terror-stricken boys in his dungeon who are unmanned by the prospect of the ghastly execution awaiting them; in the tapping out of consolatory messages whereby the desolation of Kassner's cell in *Days of Wrath* is eased and made bearable; in the descent-from-the-mountain in *Man's Hope*; in the profoundly moving spectacle of the mutiny in *The Walnut Trees of Altenburg*. It is in these and many other similar moments that Malraux is by way of setting forth what it is wherewith the gulfs and abysses of our world may be filled. He wants to say that our felicity and peace are to be found nowhere but in the upbuilding of the human City and that its one norm and ordinance is that of *fraternité*—which commits us to the celebration of the sacrament of the brother. The famous Preface to *Days of Wrath* says: "It is difficult to be a man. But it is not more difficult to become one by enriching one's fellowship with other men than by cultivating one's individual peculiarities. The former nourishes with at least as much force as the latter that which makes man human, which enables him to surpass himself . . . or realize himself." And as one thinks of the career and all that it signifies in our time (of steadfastness and integrity), one feels that it is such testimony as this that, in forming the ground of his entire work, has made his very name something like a hymn in praise of the human communion.

The gifted French critic, the late Claude-Edmonde Magny, registered a certain reservation, however, in her brilliant *Esprit* article of 1948 on Malraux, for, as she maintained, the affirmations of compassion and charity and fraternity are unsubstantiated by any truly metaphysical warrant—and thus, as she said, they are "gratuitous." True, they conjure up the possibility of a kind of grandeur, but the grandeur is inexplicable. What is the *meaning* of Katow's sacrifice, of the mutinous action that occurs on the Vistula front? Something, most assuredly, is being done as an act of witness in behalf of the sacrament of the brother, but, since it is "temporally inefficacious," what can be its justification—if, as is surely the case for Malraux, "there is no life but this one"? If God is dead, what makes the sacrament of the brother a sacrament? If, as she says, "there is no *order* (in the sense of the Christian order of charity) into which a temporally inefficacious act of charity can fit," why *should* one life place itself at the disposal of another life? What is the *raison d'être*, the metaphysical or ontological rationale, for *disponibilité* or *fraternité*? And, in the absence of such a warrant, must it not, therefore, be something merely *"experimental"*? "I am concerned," she said, "not with reproaching Malraux for not being a Christian, but simply with pointing out the intellectual fragility of his position."[35]

And no doubt the position is something fragile—though, in a time of shrunken certainties, one may well wonder how wise it is to go in for the kind of close bargaining Mme. Magny was proposing to initiate. Nor is it permissible to forget that since the Enlightenment the strictest, most reliable defenders of justice and of democratic community in the modern world have been, most of them, people prompted by a reverence for the human communion no less "gratuitous" than Malraux's. But to say, as Camus did and as Malraux would, that the ethic of *fraternité* defines that "without which the world can never be but a vast solitude,"[36] to say that it is better that men should dwell together in justice and solidarity than that they should dwell alone, to say that the life of the City is more nourishing than the life of the desert—to make this kind of testimony is surely not, in the last analysis, to advance an affirmation which is *merely* "gratuitous," however unattached it may be to a fully

35. Claude-Edmonde Magny, "Malraux le fascinateur," *Esprit*, 16e année, no. 149 (Octobre 1948), p. 530.
36. Albert Camus, *Resistance, Rebellion, and Death*, trans. Justin O'Brien (New York: Alfred A. Knopf, 1961), p. 65.

developed religious position. In any event, this has been the testimony that Malraux has made his own, and, even if it be adjudged ultimately to have the kind of fragility of which Mme. Magny complained, it remains, given his extraordinary eloquence, one of the great testimonies of the age, and one which presents in the literature of our period a singularly rich account of what, most deeply, belongs to the nature of civic virtue.

3.

Auden's Way: Towards the City— from the "Suburb of Dissent"

I heard Orpheus sing; I was not quite as moved as they say.
> —Auden, "Memorial for the City"

> . . . my name
> Stands for my historical share of care
> For a lying self-made city. . . .
> > —Auden, "Prime"

> And where should we find shelter
> For joy or mere content
> When little was left standing
> But the suburb of dissent.
> —Auden, "To Reinhold and Ursula Niebuhr"

Amidst the various darkly oracular pronouncements making up the late R. P. Blackmur's lectures at the Library of Congress in the winter of 1956—*Anni Mirabiles, 1921–1925: Reason in the Madness of Letters*—there are occasional passages whose pithiness and cogency reflect the special kind of brilliance that marked this gifted critic's finest moments. And, amongst these passages, one of the most suggestive is that which invites us to think of Rilke in relation to Robert Herrick and Emily Dickinson, for the three, says Blackmur, "are nuptial poets." "Herrick marries the created world, Dickinson marries herself, Rilke creates within himself something to marry which will—which does —marry and thereby rival the real world."[1] Which is to say that Rilke makes what Wallace Stevens (in his "Esthétique du Mal") calls a "new beginning." For, given the emptiness of the heav-

. R. P. Blackmur, *Anni Mirabiles, 1921–1925: Reason in the Madness of Letters* (Washington, D.C.: Library of Congress, 1956), p. 37.

ens above and the abandonment by the gods of man's earthly abode, the fearsome task to which he felt the poet elected was that of rescuing the world from the absolute transitoriness and chaos by which, apart from the poet's ministries, it must at last be overwhelmed. And this redeeming work (*Herz-Werk*— "heart-work—as he called it) was conceived most essentially to involve not any effort to transfigure dinginess and mediocrity, so that the actual world might be newly renovated, but rather such a liberation altogether of things (*die Dinge*) from their hopelessly inert facticity as would permit them to find a new home in the inwardness of the heart. Since the Holy Ghost has disappeared and the region of our habitancy is no longer a place of grace and glory, the things and creatures of earth must be offered the one asylum that now remains—namely, that inland sanctuary remote from the exposed frontiers of the world which is provided within, by the creative largesse of the human spirit itself. What we must do, as Rilke said in a now famous letter to his Polish translator, is "to impress this fragile, transient earth so deeply, sufferingly, and passionately upon our hearts that its essence shall rise up again, 'invisible,' within us. *We are the bees of the Invisible.*"[2] As the Seventh Duino Elegy says— "Nowhere . . . will be world but within." And to answer the earth's beseechings, that its *disjecta membra* be gathered into the inwardness of the heart, is to fulfill Rilke's definition of the poet's principal office. "How other future worlds will ripen to God I do not know, but for us art is the way"[3]—and, for him, the way of art was the way of the Angel, the way of Orpheus, the way of world-building. So the poet of the *Duino Elegies* and the *Sonnets to Orpheus* does in truth show himself to be one creating "within himself something to marry which will— which does—marry and thereby rival the real world."

Indeed, it is precisely the austerity of Rilke's commitment to his angelism, to his *religio poetae*, that makes him one of the primary saints of modern literature. For the lordly assurance

2. Rainer Maria Rilke, *Briefe aus Muzot, 1921–1926* (Leipzig: Insel-Verlag, 1938), p. 334.
3. Rainer Maria Rilke, *Tagebücher aus der Frühzeit* (Leipzig: Insel-Verlag, 1942), p. 140.

with which he took it for granted that metaphysical anarchy requires the poet to be his own legislator leads us to accord him a central place in that strain of modern writers who ask, as it were, to be regarded as having been at bottom "theologians of the poetic imagination."[4] The tradition reaches back to Mallarmé and farther still to Rimbaud, and possibly even to Hölderlin and Leopardi; and, after Paul Valéry (and perhaps Juan Ramón Jiménez), it is Wallace Stevens who is the last master of this line—the great dandiacal artificer of "supreme fictions" who was claimed, above all else, by what he called the "mystical theology" of poetry.[5] This "passionately niggling nightingale," in the vast and beautiful palace for the mind which his art creates, does in fact bring the whole modern venture in absolute poetry to its absolute climax. For he asserts more radically than any of his predecessors that, given that poverty of our condition consequent upon the emptying of the heavens, the only unified realm of experience in which man may now dwell, the one *world* remaining, is the world of poetry—which, in our own late time, is "indistinguishable from the world in which we live."[6] "The final belief is to believe in a fiction, which you know to be a fiction, there being nothing else."[7] And thus the poet is the "necessary angel of earth,"[8] since it is he ("the priest of the invisible")[9] who "gives to life the supreme fictions without which we are unable to conceive of it"[10] and who, in teaching us how to perceive ("as far as nothingness permits")[11] the mysterious coruscations of Being, clears a space for the human endeavor. The poet of *Four Quartets* says (in "East Coker"), "The poetry

---

4. The phrase is Michael Hamburger's: see his *The Truth of Poetry* (New York: Harcourt Brace Jovanovich, 1969), p. 102.

5. Wallace Stevens, *The Necessary Angel: Essays on Reality and the Imagination* (New York: Alfred A. Knopf, 1951), p. 173.

6. Ibid., p. 31.

7. Wallace Stevens, "Adagia," in *Opus Posthumous* (New York: Alfred A. Knopf, 1957), p. 163.

8. Wallace Stevens, "Angel Surrounded by Paysans," in *The Collected Poems* (New York: Alfred A. Knopf, 1954), p. 496.

9. Stevens, "Adagia," in *Opus Posthumous*, p. 169.

10. Stevens, *The Necessary Angel*, p. 31.

11. Stevens, "Questions Are Remarks," in *The Collected Poems of Wallace Stevens*, p. 463.

does not matter," but the poet of *Harmonium* and *Ideas of Order* and *Transport to Summer* wants to say that nothing else matters but the poetry, wants to say indeed with Rilke (in the third sonnet of the first Orpheus cycle) that Song *is* existence (*"Gesang ist Dasein"*); and it is the extraordinary eloquence with which he makes this testimony—in some of the most beautiful and moving poems of the modern period—that prompts us to think of Stevens as the last great exemplar of that heroic attempt in literature of the past hundred years to locate anew "the heraldic center of the world" or, given (as it may be) the irreparable fracture of that center, to build a new center and, by doing so, to save us.

Now there is perhaps no major poet of the twentieth century who stands in so resolute an opposition as does W. H. Auden to that Orphic line in modern poetry which Stevens may be regarded as having brought to a kind of conclusion. As he said in an essay of the late 1940s, "How glad I am that the silliest remark ever made about poets, 'the unacknowledged legislators of the world,' was made by a poet whose work I detest."[12] And it was with a similar severity that, over the last thirty years of his career, he regularly rejected, again and again in his essays and reviews, the attempt of the Orphic-romantic movement to offer poetry "as a guide to life" and to establish "a new nonsupernatural Catholicism."[13]

It may of course be taken for granted that Auden, very early on, in his undergraduate years at Oxford in the twenties, was captivated—like most young men then aiming at a poetic vocation—by that whole view of poetry which Eliot was enforcing upon the literary world of the time. Though the specialities of stress and idiom characteristic of Auden's *Poems* (1930) are in no simple way derivative from the poet of *Prufrock*, the basic style of procedure represented by that early book clearly indicates that he, too, conceived the Wordsworthian formula—about "emotion recollected in tranquillity"—to be "an inexact for-

12. W. H. Auden, "Squares and Oblongs," in *Poets* at Work, ed. C. D. Abbott (New York: Harcourt, Brace and Co., 1948), p. 177.
13. W. H. Auden, "Mimesis and Allegory," in *English Institute Annual, 1940*, ed. Rudolf Kirk (New York: Columbia University Press, 1941), p. 17.

mula"[14] and that he, like *il miglior fabbro* of *The Waste Land*, was by way of assuming the poet to be not any sort of *vates sacer* but rather a kind of technician who manufactures an artifact of words and sounds. Nor does one find it difficult to imagine that the young Oxonian, brooding on how "In sanatoriums they laugh less and less/Less certain of cure" (Poem XVI), was ready, in quite the same way as Eliot, to respond to Matthew Arnold's word about poetry being "at bottom a criticism of life." "At bottom: that is a great way down; the bottom is the bottom" —which "few ever see."[15]

But one also suspects that Auden's never having been charmed by the Orphic vision of the poetic enterprise was a result of his literary conscience having been early formed by the kinds of lessons being laid down in those brisk manifestoes of T. E. Hulme that Herbert Read collected and published in 1924 under the title *Speculations*. Stephen Spender reports that, in their undergraduate days at Oxford, Auden was in the habit of flatly informing him and others whom he admitted to his rooms at Christ Church that a poem's subject is "only the peg on which to hang the poetry" and that the poet is merely one like a chemist who mixes "his poems out of words whilst remaining detached from his own feelings." And this young man whose preference was for a "monosyllabic, clipped, clear-cut, icy poetry"[16] was undoubtedly one who had been very greatly swayed by Hulme's declarations against the "spilt religion" of "romanticism," against that damp, high-falutin sort of poetry that's always "flying up into the eternal gases" and talking about "the infinite," that's always "moaning or whining about something or other" and refusing to be a small, hard, dry statement.[17] Indeed, for all the shifts of emphasis in theme that belong to Auden's literary pronouncements spanning a public career of more than forty

14. T. S. Eliot, "Tradition and the Individual Talent," in *Selected Essays: 1917–1932* (New York: Harcourt, Brace and Co., 1932), p. 10.
15. T. S. Eliot, *The Use of Poetry and the Use of Criticism* (London: Faber and Faber, 1933), p. 111.
16. Stephen Spender, *World within World* (London: Hamish Hamilton, 1951), p. 51.
17. See T. E. Hulme, "Romanticism and Classicism," in *Speculations*, ed. Herbert Read (London: Kegan Paul, Trench, Trubner and Co., 1936; 2d ed.).

years, what is constantly to be remarked is this insistence that the poet is "a pedestrian taking you over the ground"[18] of the quotidian, and he always wanted utterly to refuse the kind of magniloquence which says that, when every other compass has failed, it is on poetry that we must rely for the charting of a route into some brave new world.

Auden's predilection would seem in fact never to have been one for supposing that the duty of a poem is to create a world *ex nihilo* or any sort of heterocosmic alternative to the *actual* universe: its duty was, rather, always for him that of bearing "witness to the truth,"[19] and the Johnsonian refrain consistently made by his testimony (in the verse as well as in his essays) speaks of poetic art as "a mirror held up to nature"—a mirror wherein we remain in the neighborhood of (as Caliban calls it in *The Sea and the Mirror*) "the Grandly Average Place from which at odd hours the expresses leave seriously and sombrely for Somewhere,"[20] and

> . . . where Euclid's geometry
> And Newton's mechanics would account for our experience,
> And the kitchen table exists because I scrub it.[21]

Yet, despite his disbelief in anything like *la poésie pure*, Auden's insistence on the great gulf dividing "the poetical" and "the existential" was unremitting and was expressed always with a very blunt kind of pungency. For, as he conceived the matter, the "old innocent game of playing God with words"[22] "makes nothing happen"[23]—at least nothing truly serious, since poetry "does not of itself move what is serious, the will."[24] "Poetizing" is, indeed, simply a game—a difficult game no doubt but a game

18. Ibid., p. 135.

19. W. H. Auden, "Introduction," in *The Complete Poems of Cavafy*, trans. Rae Dalven (New York: Harcourt, Brace and World, 1961), p. ix.

20. W. H. Auden, "The Sea and the Mirror," in *The Collected Poetry* (New York: Random House, 1945), p. 392.

21. W. H. Auden, "For the Time Being: A Christmas Oratorio," in *The Collected Poetry*, p. 465.

22. Auden, "Squares and Oblongs," p. 179.

23. W. H. Auden, "In Memory of W. B. Yeats," in *The Collected Poetry*, p. 50.

24. Auden, "Squares and Oblongs," p. 170.

nevertheless, a form of play whose essential frivolity stands at a great distance from anything genuinely serious, since the gulf

> . . . between choosing to obey the rules of a game which it does not matter whether you play or not, and choosing to obey the rules of life which you have to live whether you like it or not and where the rules are necessary for they do not cease to exist if you disobey them but operate within you to your destruction, this gulf is so infinite that all talk about . . . games being a preparation for . . . life is misleading twaddle.[25]

And it is, of course, the Kierkegaard of *Either/Or* and *Stages on Life's Way* who is being echoed in Auden's pronouncements on the frivolity of art, for the Idea of Poetry that he advances is, essentially, but a restatement of Kierkegaard's doctrine about the "aesthetic" point of view as that of the uncommitted spectator who lives merely on the surfaces of things, wholly absorbed by the ever changing panorama of the world but viewing it from a position of neutrality which discourages his making any decisive choices or embracing any radical imperatives. "All poets," says Auden, "adore explosions, thunderstorms, tornadoes, conflagrations, ruins, scenes of spectacular carnage,"[26] for theirs is a world of play and game. So: "Art is not life and cannot be/A midwife to society"[27] or an agent in the upbuilding of the Just City.

But, though *poiesis* is "a verbal rite"[28] and thus a kind of game, it is a game which aims to be "a game of knowledge."[29] Art is not life, but, as Auden says, "it *has* life"[30]—by which he means that, in its integral and absolute formality, in its strict patterning of what Mrs. Langer would call "virtual" worlds,[31] it presents us with evocative simulacra of what our lives would be like were *they* to be set in order. And in the degree to which

25. Ibid., p. 171.
26. Ibid., p. 179.
27. W. H. Auden, "New Year Letter," in *The Collected Poetry*, p. 267.
28. See W. H. Auden, "Making, Knowing and Judging," in *The Dyer's Hand* (New York: Random House, 1962), pp. 57–58.
29. Auden, "Squares and Oblongs," p. 173.
30. W. H. Auden, "Cav & Pag," in *The Dyer's Hand*, p. 482.
31. See Susanne Langer, *Feeling and Form* (New York: Charles Scribner's Sons, 1953), *passim*.

the poet's mastery of his language enables him to reveal the plasticity of the world, to show its amenability to the shaping power of the human word, he does to that degree present us with a model of freedom, and one which, in declaring "that order is *possible*, . . . faces us with the command to make it *actual*."[32] A work of art, in other words, simply by way of its own formal order, makes a kind of analogy of that which is referred to in the second petition of the *Our Father* ("Thy Kingdom come. . . ."), and thus its effect—as "All we are not stares back at what we are"[33]—is, inevitably, in some measure indictive and admonitory: as Caliban says (in *The Sea and the Mirror*), "What else exactly *is* the artistic gift . . . if not to make you unforgettably conscious of the ungarnished offended gap between what you so questionably are and what you are commanded without any question to become. . . ."[34]

So the poem, as Auden frequently liked to say, is something like a parable. The poet confronts two shapeless, chaotic "crowds," the vast crowd of words making up the vocabulary of his inherited language and that jumbled crowd which is comprised of recollected occasions of feeling; and what he seeks to do is to fashion a verbal *society* (that is, a system whose members are optimally united into a whole whose mode of behavior is different from that of its component members) which will itself be capable of transforming the crowd of past occasions of feeling into a *community* (that is, an order whose component members, being free and equal, èxist as a unity-in-tension). And the resulting poem thus presents "an analogy"—not an imitation but an analogy—"to that paradisal state in which Freedom and Law, System and Order are united in harmony."[35] "You cannot tell people what to do, you can only tell them parables. . . ."[36] To be sure, Auden wanted to maintain (as he

32. W. H. Auden, "The Poet of the Encirclement" (a review of T. S. Eliot's *A Choice of Kipling's Verse*), in *New Republic*, vol. 109, no. 17 (25 October 1943), p. 579.
33. Auden, "The Sea and the Mirror," p. 354.
34. Ibid., p. 400.
35. W. H. Auden, "The Virgin & the Dynamo," in *The Dyer's Hand*, p. 71.
36. W. H. Auden, "Art and Psychology," in *The Arts Today*, ed. Geoffrey Grigson (London: John Lane, 1935), p. 18.

did in his inaugural lecture as Oxford's Professor of Poetry)
that poetic statement originates in the poet's encounter with
"the sacred"[37]—by which, however, he meant not to underwrite
any sort of Longinian afflatus but only to remark, if in a somewhat eccentric fashion, the necessity of the poet's having somewhere located a dimension of radical significance in relation to
which a proper weight may then be given to the various and
sundry issues of proportion and order. But the poet *qua* poet
does not undertake to be what Catholic Christianity speaks of
as a "spiritual director": he offers only, as Auden was at most
prepared to say (following Wilfred Owen), a word of "warning," and this of a highly indirect and oblique sort, through the
formal concords of his poem—that (as it was put in that famous
line which he finally excised from his poem "September 1, 1939")
"We must love one another or die."

Yet, however much Auden was inclined in theory to disavow
didactic modes of poetic statement, the parables proposed by his
poetry—from the period of his earliest publication into the middle years of his career—did entail a rather more direct commen-
tary on the human scene of his time than anything that might
have been merely an affair of his art, in its own formal order,
adumbrating the Just City. Indeed, the prodigiously clever and
intelligent young poet of *Poems* (1930), of *Look, Stranger!*
(1936), and of *Another Time* (1940) makes us feel that his primary intentions were diagnostic and pedagogical and that, facing what seemed on all sides to be general disintegration, he
wanted to see it "as the hawk sees it or the helmeted airman."
The England in which he had come into maturity—and which
he conceived to be but a microcosm of the modern West—struck
him at the beginning of the 1930s as bearing, throughout the
entire fabric of its life, the marks of seediness and decay. The
economic system had been reduced to a shambles of stoppages
and breakdown: men were without employment and were hun-
gry and without hope: everywhere there was confusion and
dismay. It was, as he observed in his book of 1930 (in poem
XXII), a time of

37. See Auden, "Making, Knowing and Judging," in *The Dyer's Hand*,
pp. 54–60.

> Smokeless chimneys, damaged bridges, rotting wharves
> and choked canals,
> Tramlines buckled, smashed trucks lying on their side
> across the rails.
> Power-stations locked, deserted. . . .

And, as he looked out upon the "civil anarchy" ruling the "dark disordered city" of the age, this exigent young critic found it difficult not to be one—like the Voltaire he was later to describe in the poem "Voltaire at Ferney" (*Another Time*)—"Cajoling, scolding, scheming." For, as he said in the XVIth poem in the book of 1930, "It is time for the destruction of error," and the Auden of that period appears to have intended his pen to be a vigorous scalpel in its probing of blunder and perfidy.

This sense of travail in a "low dishonest decade" where, as Auden said in *The Orators* (1932), "nobody is well," did not generally eventuate, however, in a poetry informed by the kinds of close social-political observations that characterize the work of such a writer of the English thirties as George Orwell. Cecil Day Lewis trenchantly remarked at the time Auden's tendency "to replace . . . the idea of the wickedness of society by the idea of the sickness of society,"[38] and, indeed, his habit of locating the source of collective distress in the failures of personal life did have the effect of giving a certain homiletical flavor to much of his early work, as social critique enforced some quasi-psychiatric lesson and this in turn a kind of Pascalian interrogation of the individual in the bleak, dreary winter of his isolateness ("So, insecure, he loves and love/Is insecure, gives less than he expects").[39] He kept, it is true, throughout these years a steady interest in the new scene presented by the ever darkening world over which the shadow of Hitler loomed—a world (as he said in the dedicatory lines to Erika Mann in *Look, Stranger!*) of "external disorders, and extravagant lies,/. . . baroque frontiers, . . . surrealist police." And he knew that the "savaging disaster" had to be met by such a force of resistance as could be mustered only by the most carefully concerted political action. But, even as he faced the worsening public realities of a time in which the

38. Cecil Day Lewis, *A Hope for Poetry* (Oxford: Basil Blackwell, 1934), p. 46.
39. W. H. Auden, *Poems* (London: Faber and Faber, 1930), p. 30.

demonic atavism of the Nazis encountered in liberal democracy nothing more than a timorous aimlessness, his deepest concerns centered not so much on the problems arising out of the mechanisms of our social living as on what he took to be the ultimate and habitual source of these problems, in the crookedness and illiberality of the human heart. By the mid-1930s he was, to be sure, prepared to acknowledge (as he did in *Look, Stranger!*) the fatuousness of his earlier belief that "one fearless kiss would cure/The million fevers," and the poem which carries this disavowal, being addressed to his friend Christopher Isherwood, bids Isherwood in his own writing to "Make action urgent and its nature clear." Yet the "Epilogue" of *Look, Stranger!* reiterates the contention that had already become a hallmark of Auden's testimony, that the menacing floods of history will be stayed only as we heed the example of those who "had unlearnt/ Our hatred, and towards the really better/World had turned their face." It is still love, in other words, which is being advocated, though now the insistence is on the necessity of a "disciplined love," a love which by concerted action takes arms against a sea of troubles and, through a collective effort, seeks to bring them to an end. And, in the "Last Will and Testament" with which he and Louis MacNeice brought their *Letters from Iceland* (1937) to a close, the hope is expressed that "the good who know how wide the gulf . . ./Between Ideal and Real" may be granted

> . . . the power to take upon themselves the guilt
> Of human action, though still as ready to confess
> The imperfection of what can and must be built. . . .[40]

Everywhere, in short, in the work Auden produced during the first decade of his career—in the poems, in the charade *Paid on Both Sides*, in the plays (*The Dance of Death, The Dog Beneath the Skin, The Ascent of F6, On the Frontier*), and in the travel books with MacNeice (*Letters from Iceland*) and Isherwood (*Journey to a War*)—though he wanted to portray the human position as a point of juncture between the public world of society and the inner world of the spirit, his major stress fell not

40. W. H. Auden and Louis MacNeice, *Letters from Iceland* (London: Faber and Faber, 1937), p. 258.

upon the events being recorded in daily newspapers "but on events and crises in the world of the moral imagination."[41]   He wanted (as the closing poem in his book of 1930 says) to

> Cover in time with beams those in retreat
> That, spotted, they turn though the reverse were great;
> Publish each healer that in city lives
> Or country houses at the end of drives;
> Harrow the house of the dead; look shining at
> New styles of architecture, a change of heart.

But though his focus was on "the muddled heart," the poetry, in its strongest moments, moved within "a mode of public eloquence"[42] and has its background in the treacheries and evasions of the age.

In *New Year Letter*, the great poem of 1941 which presents a massive summary of the central themes and issues with which he had been occupied over the previous decade, Auden says (in Part III):

> There are two atlases: the one
> The Public space where acts are done,
> In theory common to us all . . .
> The other is the inner space
> Of private ownership, the place
> That each of us is forced to own,
> Like his own life from which it's grown,
> The landscape of his will and need
> Where he is sovereign indeed,
> The state created by his acts
> Where he patrols the forest tracts. . . .

And, like his most significant poetry of the previous decade, what the *Letter* wants to do is to define the lines of relationship between these "two atlases," since Auden was convinced that there can be no true authenticity of life apart from a right understanding of the complex mutuality by which "the public space" and "the inner space" are interdependently held together.   His reflections throughout the thirties had steadily deepened his belief that you do not have disorder in the City when there is

41. John Hollander, "Auden at Sixty," in *The Atlantic*, vol. 220, no. 1 (July 1967), p. 84.
42. Ibid.

order in the private lives of individuals, that the ultimate source of collective distress is to be found in "the error bred in the bone/Of each woman and each man." And, correlatively, he had furthermore been steadily moving towards a recognition of the ineradicable historicity of man's life, of the fact that the individual is in large part the result not only of what he himself has done but the result also, perhaps even more crucially, of what others before him have been and done and thought. So, since each man's "parish of immediacy" is deeply wrought by the bequests of history, as he—midway the journey of this life[43]—undertook an appraisal of the condition and prospect of the human enterprise in the dark time of 1940, when the clouds of war were gathered over the entire world, there seemed no chance of finding "a sesame to light" except by way of canvassing anew the annals of the modern period and reassessing the whole repertoire of beliefs and philosophies, of programs and ideologies, that had prepared the impasse then in view.

New Year Letter, then, addresses itself to "the situation of our time," to the "political upheaval" with which "our lives have been coeval." In its controlling perspective, its closest allegiances are with Dante and Pascal and Kierkegaard and, among Auden's contemporaries, with such thinkers as Karl Barth and Paul Tillich and Reinhold Niebuhr. But the poem is alert to the entire European tradition (the Greeks, the Church Fathers, the medieval Scholastics, the Reformers, Spinoza, Blake, Voltaire, Baudelaire, Rimbaud, Nietzsche, Wagner, Freud), and, at the close of one "scrambling decade" and the advent of still another which seemed to promise even more perilous emergencies, its alternately grave and witty couplets intend to stretch the secular mind of our period to the very limits of its memory, the limits beyond which there shall remain nothing for it to know but that

> A day is drawing to a close . . .
> That all the special tasks begun
> By the Renaissance have been done.

True, Western liberalism did over a long period suppose that

43. *New Year Letter*—published in 1941 (London: Faber and Faber; New York: Random House—under the title *The Double Man*)—is dated "January 1, 1940" and was, therefore, written in Auden's thirty-third year (the date of his birth having been 21 February 1907).

there was some simple path to felicity, either by way of science or education or universal suffrage. But these agencies of redemption were never able finally to break the stubborn recalcitrancies of the human polity, so that, after the sudden mutation of "Old Russia . . ./Into a proletarian state," the earlier scriptures of Adam Smith and Comte and Spencer were replaced by the revelations of Marx—and, with the rise of the Soviet experiment, "Some dreamed, as students always can,/It realized the potential Man":

> We hoped: we waited for the day
> The State would wither clean away,
> Expecting the Millennium
> That theory promised us would come.
> It didn't. Specialists must try
> To detail all the reasons why. . . .

Indeed, in that late moment when the *Letter* was being written, Auden was struck by how much

> . . . even the best
> *Les hommes de bonne volonté,* feel
> Their politics perhaps unreal
> And all they have believed untrue.
> Are tempted to surrender to
> The grand apocalyptic dream. . . .

But, as he cautioned, "to surrender to/The grand apocalyptic dream" is to elect that history shall come to an end—which is precisely what the Devil desires, for abdication is confession of defeat. Nor must we, like poor Wordsworth, repent "of our last infraction" by seeking "atonement in reaction." For, in a time of shattered dreams and broken hopes, to surrender either to apocalypticism or to reactionism is to withdraw altogether from the rough, dark weathers of the historical arena. Daunted we may be by the relentlessness with which the modern age has mounted failure on failure, but at least "failures have one good result:/They prove the Good is difficult," and they provide the occasion for the necessary discovery that

> Aloneness is man's real condition,
> That each must travel forth alone
> In search of the Essential Stone. . . .

At the dawning in January 1940 of a new decade—as "Day breaks upon the world we know/Of war and wastefulness and woe"—Auden wanted, in other words, to say that, though "The New Year brings an earth afraid," one great thing may at last be coming once again to be understood, that "true democracy begins/With free confession of our sins." And thus the poem concludes with the great prayer—

> O Unicorn among the cedars,
> To whom no magic charm can lead us . . .
> O Source of equity and rest . . .
> Disturb our negligence and chill . . .
> Send strength sufficient for our day,
> And point our knowledge on its way,
> *O da quod jubes, Domine.*

Point our knowledge on its way, the poet of the *Letter* prays; and the three long poems which followed the masterly epistle of 1941—*For the Time Being* (written in 1941–42),[44] *The Sea and the Mirror* (composed between 1942 and 1944),[45] and *The Age of Anxiety* (1947)—seem, indeed, as we look back upon them today, to have been dedicated to nothing other than a pursuit of the Way, of the Way and the Truth and the Life. By now, of course, he had entered deeply into the Christian commitments toward which he had been moving at the end of the thirties. But, given the inveterate worldliness of his mind, his assent to the *skandalon* of Christianity needed to be of a piece with his facing and evaluating every alternative to the Christian faith. As it is said in *For the Time Being*,

> . . . the garden is the only place there is, but you
>   will not find it
> Until you have looked for it everywhere and found
>   nowhere that is not a desert.

All the wrong roads had to be reconnoitered again, in order that they might be clearly seen to be only blind detours. So, as he confronted the Secular City of his time and what he took to be its incompetence at probing the "unrectored chaos" of the age,

44. See B. C. Bloomfield and Edward Mendelson, *W. H. Auden—A Bibliography, 1924–1969* (Charlottesville: The University Press of Virginia, 1972; 2d ed.), p. 51.
45. Ibid.

though knowing full well that "Art is not life and cannot be/A midwife to society," Auden wanted nevertheless to admonish and to warn and to trouble the common peace, even if this were to risk "the preacher's loose immodest tone." And it is precisely such an effort of catechizing and cross-examination which is being brilliantly undertaken in his work of the 1940s.

In his Christmas Oratorio, *For the Time Being*, he found his "text" in the Gospel narratives and proceeded allegorically to render the anguished bafflement of men everywhere on the eve of the Second World War by analogizing it to the disquietude and confusion of the ancient world on the eve of the Nativity. Through a complex structure of choruses and solos and recitatives the Oratorio takes us back into that remote time where, then as now, the type of the average man—whose mantelpiece clock had "nothing to recommend"—wanted nothing to happen. But a strange, new reality, an absolute miracle, was destined by way of a Manger to come into Caesar's disconsolate world, and the drama of *For the Time Being* is an affair of the account it gives of the ambivalence and evasion that this miracle on all sides prompted—in Joseph, who was fearful of having been cuckolded; in the Wise Men, who followed the star unto Bethlehem only because their previous journeys had proved to be merely detours into failure; in Herod, the liberal bureaucrat, who angrily resented the intrusion of radical absurdity (the notion of the Word made flesh, of the God-Man) into his rational world; in the choralists who wanted to rest in the security of a world arranged and managed for them by the great all-powerful Caesar. And, of course, in the manner of Baudelaire's famous apostrophe, the poem wants to say: "You!" "*Hypocrite lecteur! —mon semblable,—mon frère!*" Then, after the whole pageant has concluded with the flight into Egypt, the Narrator brings us back into our own present, into the world of "the moderate Aristotelian city/Of darning and the Eight-Fifteen," the world of "the time being"—which, as we are told, we shall redeem from insignificance only by following "Him through the Land of Unlikeness," only by seeking "Him in the Kingdom of Anxiety," only by loving "Him in the World of the Flesh."

In *The Sea and the Mirror*, still another essay in histrionic

116

exposition and one of the great triumphs of Auden's art, he found his "text" in Shakespeare's *The Tempest*. And, here—as he dazzlingly displays his command of sapphics and elegiacs, of terza rima and the ballade, of the sestina and the villanelle— this poet, among the most consummately gifted artists in the entire history of English poetry and one of the towering masters of the word in the modern period, wants (in the spirit of his own master, Søren Kierkegaard) to warn us against trusting to the sorceries and enchantments of art for any ultimate redemption of our human estate. In the Shakespearean pastoral, Prospero, the duke of Milan, has been banished from his realm through collusion between his traitorous brother Antonio and Alonso, the king of Naples; and we find him dwelling in retirement with his daughter Miranda, somewhere in the Mediterranean between Tunis and Naples, on a lovely island the only other inhabitant of which is a strange, half-human creature named Caliban, whom Prospero holds in servitude. Since he is a master of conjuration and wizardry, when he learns through his divining arts that a ship bearing his enemies is in the neighborhood of his coast, he prepares a storm as a means of causing the ship to founder on the island's shore. And with the help of Ariel, the angelic sprite who performs his bidding, he then proceeds to arrange a drama of judgment, of forgiveness, and of reconciliation whereby, in the end, he is restored to his dukedom and all the estrangements that had ruptured his circle are healed, the lone final recidivist being the depraved Caliban on whose nature nurture cannot stick. So Auden takes Prospero to be a "personified type of the creative," to be indeed (most especially in his alliance with Ariel, who is but a metaphor of Imagination) the very type and example of the artist, of him who transmutes the discordancies of human existence into patterns of harmony and order. And through the elaborate conceit of his masque—which involves in effect Shakespeare's curtain being lifted for the sake of allowing his characters a final speech and of inviting speculation as to how in truth they will henceforth fare—Auden attempts to take some measure of how rough in fact Prospero's "rough magic" really is. For, after "inveigling Caliban into Ariel's kingdom" and revealing its incapacity to deal with this "intrusion of the real," it then lets "loose Ariel in Caliban's" realm—but Caliban stands not for "a dream amenable to magic but [for] the all too solid flesh" of the human actuality in its elemental waywardness and intractability. Hence it is given to Caliban himself to remind us—through the long, rolling periods of his Jamesian rhetoric—of how inadequately "the mirror of art" reckons with "the sea" of reality, that sea out onto which Shakespeare's cast had finally to launch in their journey back from the magic isle to "the Grandly Average Place" in Milan and Naples where they had once again to enter into the human condition. "'Art is not life and cannot be/A midwife to society.'"

And it is in his "baroque eclogue" of 1947, *The Age of Anxiety,* that, after *New Year Letter,* we get the fullest account in his poetry of the forties of what was Auden's conception of the fundamental drift of contemporary society. The poem is a sequence of monologues and conversations and songs loosely organized (by a half-dozen "scenes") into a drama of quest and pilgrimage. But this eclogue presents no idyll of shepherds in a bucolic setting, and the poem may indeed be said to be an eclogue only perhaps in the sense carried by the Greek root (*eklegein*—to choose) from which the term derives—in the sense, that is, of its being a poem which explores a certain problem of choice, or the pathos consequent upon a certain paralysis of the capacity for making significant choices. We are taken into a New York bar on an All Souls' Night during the period of the Second World War, and there we meet four persons—the tired and aging widower, Quant, now hopelessly entrapped in the failed life of a shipping-office clerk; Malin, a middle-aged medical intelligence officer in the Canadian Air Force on a few days of leave in Manhattan; Emble, a young Midwesterner in the Navy, who suffers "that anxiety about . . . his future which haunts, like a bad smell, the minds of most young men"; and Rosetta, an English *émigrée* now prospering as a buyer for a large department store. They sit on their bar stools, each listening to the radio's orchestration of news bulletins and inane commercials and each in inward musings trying to parse the grammar of a particular loneliness and of the inchoate yearnings it gives rise to. Once they fall into a casual camaraderie, they move into a booth with their drinks; and, there, the conversation— through its hollow periphrases and its broken, heavily alliterative lines—traverses the "seven ages" of man, from the baffled helplessness of childhood to the baffled hopelessness of old age and death. And, as they reflect on how elusive is "the route/ Into hope and health," they launch into a second journey, now not across the "seven ages" but across the "seven stages" leading unto the Good Place. This voyage brings the pilgrims at last to "the hermetic gardens," there where "The ruined rebel is recreated/And chooses a chosen self." The charm and stillness of these gardens, however, is like an accusation: so they move on, and, since they have neither the faith nor the courage required to cross that dry region marking the seventh stage, "the world from which their journey had been one long flight [again] rises up before them." And, as they travel across the city by taxi to Rosetta's apartment for a snack and a nightcap, the poem sounds a dirge that speaks about how the creaking and cracking of our "world-engine" betrays the need for another miracle of healing and grace. This little group, now half-seas over, amidst the coziness of Rosetta's flat tipsily imagines that "love" may be the answer, as it is noticed that she and Emble are becoming attracted to each other: so Quant and Malin discreetly take their departure. But, after accompanying them to the elevator, Rosetta, on reentering the apartment, finds that Emble has passed out in her bedroom. "Blind on the bride-bed, the bridegroom snores,/Too aloof to love." And, as Quant sullenly makes his way homeward through the empty streets, Malin in his subway train sadly reflects on the futility of this evening of "vaguely disquieting adventures" and on the heartache that must be suffered by those who are

> unwilling to say Yes
> To the Self-So which is the same at all times,
> That Always-Opposite which is the whole subject
> Of our not-knowing, yet from no necessity
> Condescended to exist and to suffer death
> And, scorned on a scaffold, ensconced in His life
> The human household.

These four, in short, exemplify the world of the Slump: they dwell in a wilderness of their own contriving and make manifest the diminution of spirit suffered in a time whose sign is that of the *désacralisé*.

Fifteen years ago the English poet, Philip Larkin, began an essay on Auden by suggesting that, in a discussion between one man who knew only his work prior to 1940 and another who knew only the work produced after that date, it would be inevitable that "a mystifying gap" should open between them.[46] And the burden of Mr. Larkin's argument—that the post-1940 phase expressed a great falling off in animation and cogency—entailed an attempt at defining what the nature of this gap would be. The essay is not untouched by animus and wrongheadedness, but its experiment in trying to imagine such a conversation as it proposed is more than a little suggestive, for, when one takes a broad view of the *oeuvre* representing Auden's total achievement, it does most assuredly seem to fall into two major phases, though the watershed separating the one from the other is to be located not, as Mr. Larkin alleged, at the beginning of the forties but rather at the end of the decade. In a conversation, in other words, between one who knew Auden's poetry only through *The Age of Anxiety* and another who knew only his work from *Nones* (1951) on—in such a conversation, the mystifying gap that would open would be very large indeed.

The penultimate poem in *Poems* of 1930 begins by saying, "Consider this . . ."—and then, after remarking a "cigarette-end smouldering on a border/At the first garden party of the year," it goes on, like a roving camera eye, to notice the international set in winter at a sports hotel ("easy, in furs, in uniform/And constellated at reserved tables"), impoverished farmers sitting in their "kitchens in the stormy fens," the decadent insipidity of the academic cloisters ("Amid rustle of frocks and stamping feet/They gave the prizes to the ruined boys"), highborn gentlemen in their limousines "humming down arterial roads"—all this and more seen panoramically, "As the hawk sees it or the helmeted airman": it is (the English scene at the time of the Crash)

46. See Philip Larkin, "What's Become of Wystan?," in *The Spectator*, no. 6890 (15 July 1960), pp. 104–5.

a world of "strangled orchards" and "diseased youngsters," of "classic fatigue" and spreading decay. "Consider this and in our time/. . . ." And it is a similar injunction being sounded by the Auden of *The Orators* and *Look, Stranger!*, of *Another Time* and *New Year Letter*, of *For the Time Being* and *The Sea and the Mirror* and *The Age of Anxiety*—"Consider this. . . ."

Which is to say that, through the first twenty years of his poetic life, Auden's policy was that of launching—sometimes playfully, sometimes mordantly—a direct assault on a civilization and a cultural polity that, in his sense of the matter, represented failure. Stephen Spender has recorded his suspicion that, in the early years of his career, Auden's "secret fantasy of the poet" resembled "Cocteau's image in *Orphée* of Death as the surgeon with white coat and rubber gloves."[47] He was, of course, always "a marvellous talker, with all the gifts of an orator at his finger-tips,"[48] and, over a long period, the spirited and brilliant talk carried on by his poetry was that of one bent on diagnosing and arraigning and instructing a delinquent age. In an essay of 1940 in which he was setting forth the respects in which he felt Thomas Hardy to be his "poetical father," he said that what he "valued most in Hardy . . . was his hawk's vision, his way of looking at life from a very great height. . . ."[49] And it was a similar vantage point that he himself had wanted to win, for it was "time for the destruction of error," and, if the crucial faults and infirmities were to be ferreted out with clinical precision, one needed to attain and to keep something like the aerial view of "the helmeted airman."

As he looked down from a great height on the unstable world of his time, his focus did, of course, periodically shift from one to another phase of the general "crisis and dismay." In the early poems he was frequently preoccupied with the "underground proliferation of mould" that lay beneath a society of frozen credit and tottered combines, of "rotting wharves and choked canals," where what was required was "death . . ./Death of the

47. Stephen Spender, "The Life of Literature," in *Partisan Review*, vol. 15, no. 11 (November 1948), p. 1207.
48. Barbara Everett, *Auden* (Edinburgh: Oliver and Boyd, 1964), p. 25.
49. W. H. Auden, "A Literary Transference," in *The Southern Review*, vol. 6, no. 1 (Summer 1940), p. 83.

old gang." Sometimes, as it seemed, "the error" was to be located not in the malfunction of social-political structures but in the evasions of the individual, and thus he would interrogate those "nervous people who will never marry," choosing instead to live on dividends in lonely cottages, "With an animal for friend or a volume of memoirs." Then, again, the poetry would move within the world of "the flat ephemeral pamphlet and the boring meeting" and stare at "Imperialism's face/And the international wrong." And, recurrently, it would sound its summons to "build the Just City." But, whatever may have been his particular interest at a given moment, the young poet of *Poems* (1930) and *Look, Stranger!* and *Another Time* was a specialist in cultural diagnostics for whom the great idea, as Mr. Spender says, was "Symptom and Cure."[50] Or, when he was not (in Geoffrey Grigson's phrase) a "benign wizard casting out devils,"[51] he was playing the part of Schoolmaster unto his age, saying with raised forefinger, "Consider this. . . ."

Auden's poetry of the forties, it is true, records a very profound shift in basic perspective. For, as he moved from *New Year Letter* into the period of his Christmas Oratorio and *The Sea and the Mirror* and *The Age of Anxiety*, it became apparent that no longer was he under the tutelage of his earlier mentors, of Freud and (more remotely) Marx, of Georg Groddeck and Homer Lane and D. H. Lawrence. His progress had at last brought him onto the terrain of the Christian faith into which, indeed, he was to enter even more deeply throughout the remaining thirty years of his career; and the guides presiding over this *metanoia* were such figures as Augustine and Pascal and Kierkegaard, Reinhold Niebuhr and Paul Tillich and Charles Williams. Yet, now as a Catholic obedient to Anglican tradition, the distinguishing style of his speech and thought did in no way undergo any significant alteration, for he kept his old belief that the "duty of a poem . . . is to bear witness to the truth": as he faced the secular forums of his day from the standpoint of his newly embraced orthodoxy, the central stress of his poetry continued to

50. Stephen Spender, "W. H. Auden and His Poetry," in *The Atlantic Monthly*, vol. 192, no. 1 (July 1953), p. 75.
51. Geoffrey Grigson, "Auden as a Monster," in *New Verse*, nos. 26–27 (November 1937), p. 15.

be aggressive, polemical, admonitory—and the note of trium-
phalism is often to be heard in the undertones of his work of
the 1940s, as when he is bidding us to make "free confession of
our sins" and (as his "Star of the Nativity" says in *For the Time
Being*) to

> Descend into the fosse of Tribulation,
> Take the cold hand of Terror for a guide.

In *Nones*, his book of 1951, and *The Shield of Achilles*, which
followed it in 1955, a new poetic personality, however, began
to make itself felt, and this even more decidedly so through the
sixties and early seventies in Auden's last books—in *Homage to
Clio* (1960), *About the House* (1965), *City without Walls*
(1969), *Epistle to a Godson* (1972), and the posthumous volume of 1974 *Thank You, Fog*. In these wonderfully nuanced
and deeply affecting volumes of his full maturity, his extraordinary adroitness in the management of meter and diction and
syntax continues, of course, to be the prodigy it had always been,
and, as he goes about his elaborately mannerist procedures, he
remains one who (as he puts it in one of the finest poems in *The
Shield of Achilles*—"'The Truest Poetry is the most Feigning'")
wants to say to himself

> Be subtle, various, ornamental, clever,
> And do not listen to those critics ever
> Whose crude provincial gullets crave in books
> Plain cooking made still plainer by plain cooks,
> As though the Muse preferred her half-wit sons. . . .

But the old pugnacious, bullying, vigilant strictness is gone, or
does at least now come to the force only very rarely. He is still
"a marvellous talker," but the talk being heard in the late poetry
is the quiet, equable, urbanely courteous talk of one who has
chosen for his *ars poetica* "the wry, the sotto-voce,/Ironic and
monochrome." And, in his late books, the caustic, imperious,
exigent wittiness of an earlier period has deepened down into
a profoundly comic compassionateness and equanimity. Here,
it is no longer the "hawk's vision" that he covets, for he has come
to realize (as he says in the beautifully composed "Memorial
for the City" in *Nones*) that

> The steady eyes of the crow and the camera's candid eye
> See as honestly as they know how, but they lie.

"The eyes of the crow and the eye of the camera open/Onto Homer's world, not ours." And Homer's world, as he had earlier said in an essay on Greek culture,

> . . . is unbearably sad because it never transcends the immediate moment; one is happy, one is unhappy, one wins, one loses, finally one dies. That is all. Joy and suffering are simply what one feels at the moment; they have no meaning beyond that; they pass away as they came; they point in no direction; they change nothing. It is a tragic world but a world without guilt for its tragic flaw is not a flaw in human nature, still less a flaw in an individual character, but a flaw in the nature of existence.[52]

Homer's world, therefore, is not the world in which we dwell: as the "Memorial" reminds us,

> Our grief is not Greek: As we bury our dead
> We know without knowing there is reason for what we bear,
> That our hurt is not a desertion, that we are to pity
> Neither ourselves nor our city;
> Whoever the searchlights catch, whatever the loudspeakers blare,
> We are not to despair.

Which is to say that, since we are hobbled neither by some essential defect in the nature of existence nor by some inherent defect in the nature of the human faculty, our tears need never be tears of self-pity but only tears of remorse and repentance. So the detached, objective, aerial view—of the crow and the camera, of the hawk and the helmeted airman—does not, in the end, afford a proper perspective on our human condition: it may, from its altitude, offer a fair prospect of the craggy, mountainous uplands of the world, but, in the late poems, Auden wants to say that the scene "Of green and civil life" (as *New Year Letter* calls it) is the

> . . . places where we have really been, dear spaces
>   Of our deeds and faces, scenes we remember
> As unchanging because there we changed, where shops have names,
>   Dogs bark in the dark at a stranger's footfall

52. "Editor's Introduction," in *The Portable Greek Reader*, ed. W. H. Auden (New York: Viking Press, 1948), p. 20.

And crops grow ripe and cattle fatten under the kind
    Protection of a godling or goddessling
Whose affection has been assigned them, to heed their needs and
    Plead in heaven the special case of their place.[53]

We are, in short, imperfect, conditioned, earthbound creatures; and, however far we may venture out beyond our wonted
precincts or however high we may climb those treacherous
mountains that Hopkins called "cliffs of fall" ("Frightful, sheer,
no-man-fathomed"),[54] we are still of the earth and earthy. And,
in its intention to find its own fulcrum in the mundane, unexceptional region of our everyday habitancy, the poetry of Aud-
en's last years shows itself to be controlled by persistently comic
sympathies, for it is, indeed, the special tendency of the comic
vision to assert our deep, unsunderable involvement in the things
of earth, and to do this in a spirit of praise and thanksgiving.
Moreover, despite the infrequency with which the late poems
avail themselves of Christian theological concepts as an arsenal
for polemic or disputation, it may be just in their readiness to
affirm the dignity of "the ordinary universe" that they prove
how deeply formed by the perspectives of an Incarnational faith
the mind of this poet in his late maturity had come to be.

It was the great poem in *Nones*, "In Praise of Limestone,"
that presented what was perhaps the first major expression of
Auden's "late" style. He had earlier in *New Year Letter* declared his affection for those limestone moors chained by the
Pennine uplands in the countryside of northern England, identi-
fying this as the locality that came to mind whenever he tried
to imagine where it might be that "the human creature" could
perhaps best be brought "to sense and decency." And here,
in *Nones*, he explains what it is that prompts his fondness for
this landscape:

> If it form the one landscape that we the inconstant ones
>   Are consistently homesick for, this is chiefly
>   Because it dissolves in water.

53. "Air Port," in *Nones* (New York: Random House, 1951), p. 23.
54. *The Poems of Gerard Manley Hopkins*, ed. W. H. Gardner and N. H.
Mackenzie, 4th ed. (London–New York: Oxford University Press, 1967),
p. 100.

The impermanence of this limestone world is like the transiency of the human thing itself; and, furthermore, it is a "region/Of short distances and definite places," a region "Where everything can be touched or reached by walking"—"sometimes/Arm in arm, but never, thank God, in step." It is thus a place whose gently "rounded slopes/With their surface fragrance of thyme" invite us to remember how deeply rooted we are in the finite creaturality that belongs to the things of earth, to remember that we are men and not angels. Which may be why, as the poem's speaker surmises, "The best and worst never stayed here long but sought/Immoderate soils": the would-be saint is drawn to "granite wastes" and "Intendant Caesars" to clayed and gravelly plains where "there is room for armies to drill" and where "rivers/Wait to be tamed." But this calm terrain, this backward and dilapidated province, this human place, makes an analogue of the scene and site of the common life, of the well-trodden, middling world in which the generality of human-kind actually dwells. Yet, though it may be scorned by the tigers of wrath, it is not without its own peculiar power to dis-turb, for it "calls into question/All the Great Powers assume": by thrusting forward the rock-bottom earthiness of man's life and by reminding us how incorrigibly finite all human things are, it does in effect expose the fraudulence of all attempts (whether by art or by science or by religion) at leaping out of the human condition into Magnificence and Glory: "it dissolves in water" and thereby makes us remember that we must "look forward/To death as a fact." So when he tries to imagine the Good Place, says Auden, "what I hear is the murmur/Of under-ground streams, what I see is a limestone landscape."

The poem in *Nones* called "Memorial for the City," in its swift résumé of two thousand years of Christendom, reviews the great patterns of the *civitas terrena* in Western history. It recalls that New City resulting from the precarious balance of papal and imperial power—which was followed by the Sane City of the high Middle Ages, where "disciplined logicians" held at bay "the eccentricities of the private brain." This dispensa-tion, however, in due course was denounced by Luther as the Sinful City; and, amidst the fragmentations brought by Reformation and Renaissance, reason and science claimed the primacy, so that there came a time when "history marched to the drums of a clear idea" and all was aimed at the Rational City—whose shadow falls across the whole modern quest for the Conscious City, where men may be "Faithful without faith." But, as the poem wants eventually to say, the last state of things is worse than the first, for, in our own late time, the modern experiment in secularization issues only in "the abolished City," where the world seems to be "a chaos of graves" and where "the barbed-wire stretches ahead/Into our future till it is lost to sight." So, then, says Auden, *"Let Our Weakness speak,"* and this is what the concluding section of the poem wants to give voice to—the duplicity and opportunism, the recreancy and sharp practice, the mulishness and illiberality that are the despair of social engineers and all those who would build "Metropolis, that too-great city." The poem, in other words, wants finally to hold up the bloody beastliness of men—as that which has no doubt ever and again subverted the enterprise of *communitas* but which, in its very intractability, bespeaks a certain stoutness in our flesh that offers a kind of hope for the human future. And though this gritty, gamy waywardness of the race may, to be sure, exasperate those who would reduce the world to the tidiness of a chessboard, the richly ironic poem in *Nones* called "The Managers" suggests that, so far as they are concerned—the quiet men who work too hard in rooms too big, eating with one hand little luncheons of sandwiches brought in a tray while handling with the other "papers a couple/Of secretaries are needed to file"—

> . . . no one is really sorry for their
>   Heavy gait and careworn
> Look, nor would they thank you if you said you were.

Now it is this insistently comic perspective that provides the basic point of view controlling not only "In Praise of Limestone" and "Memorial for the City" and "The Managers" but also many of the other poems in *Nones*—among them, "Their Lonely Betters" (with its strikingly devised echoes of Robert Frost), "Ischia," "Pleasure Island," "Under Which Lyre." It is a poetry carrying much complexity of theme and argument, but—in its colloquial idioms, its easy mingling of wit and gravity, its relaxed conversational tone, its preference for loosely stressed accentual lines—studiedly avoiding the large gesture. For, as he says in the dedicatory lines "To Reinhold and Ursula Niebuhr," the language of "the grand old manner," of the "resonant heart," is "soiled, profaned, debased" and has been too much used "to befuddle the crowd." So, in the elected manner of his oblique informality, Auden's great technical virtuosity begins in his poetry of the fifties to be dedicated to an essentially comic work, of declaring amidst the ruins of the Rational City that, however intractable the Managers may find the human reality to be, there is, just in its very recalcitrancy and waywardness, a kind of sign, a sign of a certain obstinate sturdiness in things—in the scents of flowers and the songs of birds, as well as in the frowardness of men—that no rationalist technicism can bring to heel. And thus, in the spirit of that sense of deep encouragement which ensued, he was moved to make the great testimony voiced by the poem in *Nones* called "Precious Five":

> I could . . .
> Find reasons fast enough
> To face the sky and roar
> In anger and despair
> At what is going on,
> Demanding that it name
> Whoever is to blame:
> The sky would only wait
> Till all my breath was gone
> And then reiterate
> As if I wasn't there
> That singular command
> I do not understand,
> Bless what there is for being. . . .

Indeed, what is most remarkable in the books of Auden's last years—in *The Shield of Achilles,* in *Homage to Clio,* in *About the House,* in *City without Walls* and *Epistle to a Godson*—is this Blakean impulse by which they are all touched, the impulse to celebrate and doxologize the holiness of the world. And they are books in which the world is being looked at not through the narrow end of the telescope, where the view is of the enormous and dreadful abysm of existence: things instead are being looked at through the larger end of the instrument—which is, of course (as Fr. William Lynch reminds us), the comic stand-point, where "everything has become not sea incarnadine but a disconcertingly small puddle."[55] Auden's telescope, in short, is turned around: so it brings into view the common, average, ordinary circumstances and realities of life, and it is in these that holiness is descried.

It should not, therefore, be considered odd that many of the late poems are focused on pastoral themes and situations, for, when a poet so deeply steeped in urban ethos as Auden always was begins to reflect on the sustaining continuities of the quotidian realm, it is no doubt to be expected that he (perhaps most especially he) will feel an impulse to recall the various supportive agencies in the natural order by which human life is upborne. And, indeed, the poems of Auden's last years are recurrently to be found performing rites of homage to that good lady, Dame Kind—"our Mum"—who, Coarse Old Party that she is, keeps all the vitalities of nature unimpaired. For She gives our bodies their solid structures of bone which "Are no discredit to our kind." She gives us hands which "reckon, beckon, demonstrate," so that, even when we wander in foreign lands, "We command a rhetoric/Which makes us glad we came." And we are indebted to Her not only for the marvelously pleasurable and efficient "corporal contraptions" we are but also for all the wonderfully variegated creatures and processes that form the environing theatre of our life in the world, things so astonishing in their power to nourish and to heal that this poet, with his old propensity for parables, was moved again and again in the latter phase of his career to proffer one or another kind of parable recording a meditation initiated by some wonderment at the miraculous prodigality and beneficence of the order administered by Dame Kind. The *pietas*, expressed always wryly and *sotto voce*, is not at all Wordsworthian—five minutes of gazing at some vista in the Lake District would be "awfully long"—but, for all the ironic qualifications with which it may hedge itself about, it is something very deeply felt.

55. William F. Lynch, S.J., *Christ and Apollo: The Dimensions of the Literary Imagination* (New York: Sheed and Ward, 1960), p. 94.

Auden's pastoral mode attains one of its finest expressions in the sequence of seven poems in *The Shield of Achilles* entitled "Bucolics." In "Winds," inscribed not surprisingly to Alexis Léger (St.-John Perse), he reminds us that the agitated airs of the world "make weather," and he prays that, in all seasons and all weathers, the Goddess of winds will grant that he, her clerk and minstrel, may so perform "every verbal rite" as to make it an act of "anamnesis/Of what is excellent" in all the things and creatures of earth. The iambic pentameters of "Woods" challenge the old convention that opposes the decorum of human society to the murder and rapine of sylvan thickets; and they suggest that the world's forest tracts (which are often to be found "massacred to the last ash") are in fact at the mercy of men, that their condition reveals "a lot about a country's soul"—"A culture is no better than its woods." "Mountains" speaks a word of warning against "steep places" which may attract "unsmiling" men reaching after Heaven but which do not make a good terrain for most of us, "uncatlike" as we are. Similarly, "Lakes" also expresses a preference for the small, domiciliated scale of things:

> A lake allows an average father, walking slowly,
> To circumvent it in an afternoon,
> And any healthy mother to halloo the children
> Back to her bedtime from their games across:
> (Anything bigger than that, like Michigan or Baikal,
> Though potable, is an 'estranging sea').

"Islands," in its brisk and witty quatrains, catalogues the various types who dwell on keys and island shelfs—saints on millstones, pirates in their lairs, convicted criminals, exiled emperors—but the poem insists that the broad majority of men must find "a mainland livelihood." In "Plains," the poet confesses that he cannot see a stretch of flats—"where all elsewheres are equal" and where all "roads run level"—"without a shudder," though, as he recalls how he has often lost his way in valleys and lowlands, he also admits that perhaps "I've reason to be frightened/ Not of plains . . . but of me." Then, in "Streams," the last and most beautiful of these eclogues, he speaks of that for which he has the greatest affection, "clear water," convivial and cheering in all its streams, seeming always "glad—though goodness knows why—to run with the human race":

> as you dash or loiter through life who does not love
> > to sit beside you, to hear you and see you,
> > pure being, perfect in music and movement?
>
> Air is boastful at times, earth slovenly, fire rude,
> but you in your bearing are always immaculate,
> > the most well-spoken of all the older
> > servants in the household of Mrs. Nature.

It should be apparent, then, that in these essays in *paysage moralisé*, as in his numerous other poems in a bucolic mode, Auden does not permit himself any kind of arcadian sentimentality. For the natural order that he confronts, though finally inviting homage and reverence, presents itself at least initially in the form of moral ambiguity, besmudged as it is with all the improprieties of men. Nor does his tutelage under the great masters of Christian anthropology ever allow him to suppose that there is some balm in nature that offers a quick and easy cure for the ailments of the human heart. Indeed, the great sequence of poems with which *The Shield of Achilles* concludes—"Horae Canonicae"—wants to insist on how incontrovertibly and inexorably, throughout all the rhythms of each daily round, we are as much implicated in the crucifixion of Christ as were those who nailed him to his cross on that Friday afternoon of long ago.

This cycle of seven texts, as its title indicates, offers a series of meditations marking those seven Canonical Hours that are laid down by the old breviaries of the Western Church as the times for saying the offices of daily prayer. "Prime" (6 a.m.) speaks of that moment at the beginning of the day when, "Recalled from the shades to be a seeing being," the self wakes to consciousness, still—in the moment of waking—"wholly in the right." But no sooner does the body stir into its first movements than "this ready flesh" becomes the accomplice and the creature of the will—whose inveterately self-regarding motivation immediately ordains that "I" shall *fall* into "my historical share of care/For a lying self-made city"; and thus, as the poem suggests, to "draw breath . . . is . . . to die."

By 9 a.m. ("Terce") "I" will have shaken the paws of my dog, quietly closed the door of my wife's bedroom on one of her headaches, and started off on the day's affairs, with such a prayer as—

> 'Let me get through this coming day
> Without a dressing down from a superior,
> Being worsted in a repartee,
> Or behaving like an ass in front of the girls;
> Let something exciting happen,
> Let me find a lucky coin on a sidewalk.
> Let me hear a new funny story.'

(But by sundown "I" "shall have had a good Friday," shall have managed, however obscurely or unimpressively situated my life may be, to have dealt another blow to the fearfully bruised face of Christ.)

By noon ("Sext"), indeed, the great machine of the world's business is awhir, and you will find "a cook mixing a sauce, a surgeon/making a primary incision,/a clerk completing a bill of lading"—all wearing "the same rapt expression,/forgetting themselves in a function." And, apart from the various technical specialists and functionaries who perform the work of civilization, there is the *fourmillante cité* which sees only what the crowd can see and "only believes in that/in which there is only one way of believing."

By three o'clock in the afternoon we are well into the heat of the day, and "Nones" is set therefore in the siesta hour, when "the faceless many" lie sprawled in slumber, none able now to "remember why/He shouted or what about/So loudly in the sunshine this morning." This, in the chronology of the New Testament narrative, is the time that followed the Crucifixion, when indeed "the faceless many" then, if challenged, would have replied:

> —'It was a monster with one red eye,
> A crowd that saw him die not I.'—

So now, as then, their "projects under construction,/Look only in one direction." "The shops will re-open at four": meanwhile, there is "time/To misrepresent, excuse, deny,/Mythify" that event which occurred at the Place of a Skull and which is re-enacted over and again each day in all the other places of man's habitation.

"Vespers" brings us to the time of early evening (6 p.m.), and, here, "in this hour of civil twilight," Auden's speech relaxes into a prose idiom, as "two paths cross"—that of "an Arcadian" (who is the speaker) and that of "a Utopian":

> Neither speaks. What experience could we possibly share?
> Glancing at a lampshade in a store window, I observe it is too hideous for anyone in their senses to buy: He observes it is too expensive for a peasant to buy.
> Passing a slum child with rickets, I look the other way: He looks the other way if he passes a chubby one. . . .
> You can see, then, between my Eden and his New Jerusalem, no treaty is negotiable.

Yet this encounter is "also a rendezvous between two accomplices," since their Victim is one "on whose immolation" both arcadias and utopias are founded: which is to say that, when all the relativities of our tastes and perspectives are viewed in relation to the Primal Fact (of, in the Evangelist's phrase, the "ransom for the many" that sinlessness was required to pay), they prove to be relativities that do not entail any very great difference.

"Compline" marks the hour (9 p.m.) when the day is over and when one would like to be able, in an "instant of recollection," to shape its happenings into some pattern of significance—but all that can be recalled

> are doors banging,
> Two housewives scolding, an old man gobbling,
> A child's wild look of envy,
> Actions, words, that could fit any tale. . . .

And, as the poem's speaker tellingly admits, "I cannot remember/A thing between noon and three" (the time of the Crucifixion). But, as he gradually lapses into sleep, a prayer (from the Ordinary of the Mass) is wrung from his lips—"*libera me*" —and, "in the name of a love/Whose name one's forgotten," he asks that the time may come when he "shall know exactly what happened . . . between noon and three."

So it is a very stringent measure indeed that Auden was prepared to take of that "village of the heart" wherein "ordinary decent folk," with all their transgressions and evasions, daily dwell. Yet it is in these inglorious precincts, amidst the commonplace mutualities of the human household, that we are summoned to be obedient to the requirements of *agape*: as Justin Replogle reminds us, Auden shared with Robert Frost the conviction that "The earth's the right place for love."[56] But there shall be no love on earth unless the things and creatures of earth themselves are loved: so "Lauds," the beautiful lyric which brings the "Horae" to an end, as it listens at dawn to the warbling of small birds and the crowing of the cock, sings out its imploration:

> God bless the Realm, God bless the People;
> God bless this green world temporal. . . .

Now it is the great canticle with which the "Horae" conclude ("God bless this green world temporal") that, from our present vantage point, may be seen to have prefigured the line Auden would be taking in the work of his last years. For in the collection of his poems that he issued in 1960, *Homage to Clio*, and in the book that followed it five years later, *About the House*, it is, indeed, Clio who (as in the later volumes also) is his Muse. She is, of course, the goddess of time, the guardian-spirit who presides over our steady passage through all the finite, limited moments of our journey amidst "this green world." And whenever we are seized by any "angelic" passion for some specious "eternity" and are thus prompted to conceive these finite, limited moments as something to break out of and to be escaped from, it is a part of Clio's office to arrange for us to be reminded that our residence is not in the heavens, that we are irrevocably committed to the ordinary, unexceptional world of our earthbound career, and that we had, therefore, better learn to take our lives on the terms of their concrete actuality. So it is appropriate that Clio, unlike Artemis and Aphrodite, should be one for whom the arts have no ready icon, that she (as Auden says) should "look like any/Girl one has not noticed"—for, as the goddess of time, her special realm is that of the quotidian; and this is precisely the region being explored in the wonderfully rich books

56. Justin Replogle, *Auden's Poetry* (Seattle: University of Washington Press, 1969), p. 170.

of Auden's final years. Here, under Clio's guidance, he is taking stock not of lords and saints but of "all poor s-o-b's who
never/Do anything properly," of those who merely breed good
horses and find decent answers to their questions, who pay their
bills promptly, and who (as the Eliot of *The Cocktail Party*
would say) keep the hearth. His Representative Man is he
who, however audacious and far-ranging his nocturnal dreams,
finds himself condemned (or privileged) to be only human and
who—Voice of "Our Weakness" that he is—scrapes up a sup-
portable bulwark against the mortifications of life by blessing
what there is for being, by forswearing both Paradise Losts and
New Jerusalems, by being grateful to Dame Kind that, though
"She mayn't be all she might . . . She *is* our Mum," by facing
into the fact of his commitment to time, and by being glad for
the shelter over his hèad under which, as he says, "I needn't,
ever, be at home *to*/those I am not at home *with. . . .*"

But the genial, seasoned, gray eminence that Auden had become at the end—the man who had found "an angle of experience where the dark is distilled into light" and where our daily
bumblings with work and friends may be seen to go "straight to
the key which creation was composed in"[57]—this poet (in his
desire to bless what there is for being) proved, as at times he
still does, to be for many only a disappointing backslider who
had strangely lost the prophetic rectitude of an earlier time.
The technical virtuosity of the later poems, the astounding range
of the vocabulary he commands, the clarity he manages to keep
in syntactical constructions of frequently enormous complexity,
his well-nigh unexampled genius as a metrist, the extraordinary
contrapuntalism with which he orchestrates voices and tones
(coarse heartiness, mock solemnity, circus horseplay, high eloquence), the great breadth of learning and scholarship that supports his reflections, the outrageous ease with which he turns out
odes and clerihews and villanelles and ballades and *haiku*—all
this remains as impressive as ever before. But this poet who
now finds his "catholic area" to be his living room, where friends

57. Christopher Fry, "Comedy," in *The New Orpheus: Essays toward a
Christian Poetic,* ed. Nathan A. Scott, Jr. (New York: Sheed and Ward,
1964), p. 287.

gather after dinner for music or gossip; who forswears "the preacher's loose immodest tone," believing that in our rackety and clamorous age a truly human speech must now be quiet and intimate; who obstinately focuses his later poetry, therefore, not on the public spaces of the age but on the domestic scene, where men may meet "without papers" to enjoy a good dinner; and who wants, amidst the civil amenities and formalities of the domestic life, to sound a *Benedicite*—this, in the judgment of numerous arbiters, is a poet who had given up his earlier intention to promote "new styles of architecture" and to be a "conscript to our age." Indeed, as it is sometimes charged, the Auden of *About the House* and *City without Walls* and *Epistle to a Godson*—"overdined and overwined"[58]—is one who had suffered a sad "change of life"; and the sclerosis of the last years, it is said, when viewed in relation to the insouciantly *engagé* figure of the thirties and forties, can only be taken to represent an unfortunate decline into reactionist "apoliticalism."[59]   So Philip Larkin's question of 1960—"What's become of Wystan?" —is recurrently raised, the tense now of course, unhappily, needing to be preterit.

Yet, surely, any careful reconsideration of Auden's line of progress, if not controlled by hostile bias, ought to indicate that the case is by no means so simple as it is made out to be by those who think of him as having been in his last years a Lost Leader.   And what needs particularly to be heeded in that line of progress is the steadiness with which, from the 1940s on, he ever more firmly resolved not to give his own suffrage to the ominously darkening world of the new *Masse-Mensch*.   For life in our own century, as he came more and more deeply to feel over the last twenty-five years of his career, is perilously drifting towards a polity comprised of such entities as arise when men are simply added together into the kinds of collectives that may be efficiently controlled and manipulated by the managerial élite brought to a position of world-rulership in this present post-heroic

58. François Duchene, *The Case of the Helmeted Airman: A Study of W. H. Auden's Poetry* (London: Chatto and Windus, 1972), p. 176.
59. See Richard M. Ohmann, "Auden's Sacred Awe," in *Commonweal*, vol. 78 (31 May 1963), pp. 279–81.

stage of bourgeois capitalism, at the end of the modern era.

One suspects, indeed, that Auden was very greatly influenced not only by the Kierkegaard of *Either/Or* and *Stages on Life's Way* but also by the Kierkegaard of that brilliant book of 1846 called *The Present Age*, which announced that all the basic structures of modern society are calculated to keep a man from saying "I." It is the crowd, said Kierkegaard, that is fast becoming the fundamental form of human existence. Anticipating that line of testimony which has more lately come from such thinkers as Jaspers and Ortega and Marcel and Berdyaev, he contended that the people of the modern period are no longer prepared to risk any attempt at straightforwardly reckoning with their individual selfhood: instead, they form a committee —and "in the end the whole age becomes a committee."[60] In his estimate, the result is the invasion of the world by that new phantom he called "the public"—"a kind of gigantic something, an abstract and deserted void which is everything and nothing,"[61] and which begins to come into existence when men give up their individuality for the sake of buying the cheap sort of safety to be had when one is engulfed, as an anonymous unity, into a social collective. Then, "all inwardness is lost,"[62] and the world enters into an "age of levelling."[63] And, of course—as we have been reminded again and again by that tradition of modern sociology running, say, from Georg Simmel and Max Weber to Jacques Ellul—this great indolent human mass constituting "the public" breeds that strange dispensation in which the bureaucratic ethos takes the ascendancy, where those for whom life must be something like a vast committee elect that their fate shall be conjured with by the inscrutable men comprising the cadre of Technicians, of Experts, of Managers, whose overriding concern is "to wipe out the blots . . . [that] personal determination introduces into the perfect design of the organization."[64]

60. Søren Kierkegaard, *The Present Age*, trans. Alexander Dru and Walter Lowrie (London–New York: Oxford University Press, 1940), p. 17.
61. Ibid., p. 41.
62. Ibid., p. 16.
63. Ibid., p. 33.
64. Jacques Ellul, *The Technological Society*, trans. John Wilkinson (New York: Alfred A. Knopf, 1964), p. 138.

Now it is this Myth—which, regrettably, has proved to have a remarkable power to illumine the drift of the age—that began, as it would seem, at some time in the forties to organize one phase of Auden's thought. He was not, to be sure, any sort of systematic theorist of the relations between *Gemeinschaft* and *Gesellschaft*, but the decline from the one to the other may be seen at various points to have been something he was deeply pondering over a long period. As early as 1941, in an essay entitled "Criticism in a Mass Society," he was already remarking the failure of the modern populace in the liberal democracies "to acquire the habits [of thought] that an open society demands,"[65] was remarking how much "the great majority prefer opinion to knowledge, and passively allow the former to be imposed upon them by a centralized few."[66] Or, again, in an essay of 1948 on Yeats, he said: "No private citizen to-day thinks seriously, 'Here is superior me and there are all those other people'; but 'Here are we, all in the same boat, and there is It, the Government.' "[67] Two years later, he was observing that revolutions may often be graphically represented by a symbolic figure—the American, say, by a pioneer, the French by an intellectual—and that perhaps the appropriate symbol of the revolution we are in the midst of today is "a naked anonymous baby," since

> It is for the baby's right to health, not for the freedom of any person or class to act or think—for a baby is not yet a person and cannot choose or think—that the revolution is being fought everywhere in one way or another. A baby has to be controlled, it has to be indoctrinated, it cannot be told more of the truth than it can profitably understand, so the present revolution is authoritarian and believes in censorship and propaganda. Since its values are really derived from medicine, from a concept of health, it is hostile to any nonconformity, any deviation from the norm. . . .
>
> What will happen is anybody's guess. Perhaps history is forcing the intellectual, whether scientist or artist, into a new conception of himself as neither the respectable bard nor the

65. W. H. Auden, "Criticism in a Mass Society," in *The Intent of the Critic*, ed. Donald A. Stauffer (Princeton: Princeton University Press, 1941), p. 129.

66. Ibid., p. 127.

67. W. H. Auden, "Yeats as an Example," in *The Kenyon Review*, vol. 10, no. 2 (Spring 1948), p. 191.

anarchic aesthete, but as a member of the Loyal Opposition, defending, not for his own sake only but for all, the inalienable rights of the individual person against encroachment by an over-zealous government, with which, nevertheless, even though the latter deny it, he has a bond, their common love for the Just City.[68]

Nor does one have any difficulty at all in adjusting to this kind of argument such a poetic statement as "The Managers" (in *Nones*) makes, about those for whom "there will be places on the last/Plane out of disaster"—the New Men who have "The last word on how we may live or die,"

> Men, working too hard in rooms that are too big,
>   Reducing to figures
> What is the matter, what is to be done.
>   A neat little luncheon
> Of sandwiches is brought to each on a tray,
>   Nourishment they are able
> To take with one hand without looking up
>   From papers a couple
> Of secretaries are needed to file,
>   From problems no smiling
> Can dismiss. . . .

And a large number of similar citations may be gathered from Auden's writings of the fifties and sixties, from both his poems and his essays.

In the whole course of his reflections in this vein, it was no doubt his reading of Hannah Arendt's *The Human Condition*[69] that constituted a major event, and one finds it surprising that, among those who have attempted to reckon with Auden's late phase, it is Richard Johnson alone who has sensed the depth of Miss Arendt's impact.[70] The very careful review of the book

68. W. H. Auden, "Introduction," *Poets of the English Language*, ed. W. H. Auden and Norman Holmes Pearson, vol. 5 (New York: Viking Press, 1950), p. xxv.

69. Hannah Arendt, *The Human Condition* (Chicago: University of Chicago Press, 1958); the quotations which follow are from the "Collector's Edition" (Fifth Impression), published in 1969.

70. See Richard Johnson, *Man's Place: An Essay on Auden* (Ithaca: Cornell University Press, 1973), pp. 213–16 and pp. 224–25. And, in this connection, it may not be insignificant that the magnificent collection of Auden's essays and reviews, *Forewords and Afterwords* (New York: Random House), published in the spring of 1973, a few months before his death, is dedicated to Hannah Arendt.

that Auden published in the English magazine *Encounter* was obviously the result of enormous pains having been taken to master the great complexities of her dialectic; and it is not unlikely that *The Human Condition* requires to be associated with that select group of books—Kierkegaard's *Stages on Life's Way*, Charles Williams's *He Came Down from Heaven*, Charles Norris Cochrane's *Christianity and Classical Culture*, Reinhold Niebuhr's *The Nature and Destiny of Man*, Denis de Rougemont's *L'Amour et l'Occident*—which, beyond all others, must be taken account of in any comprehensive plotting of his mature thought. Indeed, as he said in his review, "Every now and then, I come across a book which gives me the impression of having been especially written for me. In the case of a work of art, the author seems to have created a world for which I have been waiting all my life; in the case of a 'think' book, it seems to answer precisely those questions which I have been putting to myself. . . . Miss Hannah Arendt's *The Human Condition* belongs to this small and select class. . . ."[71]

In her book of 1958 Miss Arendt's subject remained what it had been in the book by which, seven years earlier, she had first won a large reputation, *The Origins of Totalitarianism*—though, now, she was concerned not with the kind of outrageous despotism fostered by Stalin and Hitler but, rather, with that equally virulent tyrannizing of the human spirit which is effectuated in the modern period by the totalitarianism of mass society. In the terms of Miss Arendt's own lexicon, however, the familiar locution "mass society" would need to be denominated a redundancy, for what she takes to be the great distinguishing fact of the modern scene is "the emergence of the social realm,"[72] the rise to ascendancy of a type of consociation amongst men whereby they are related to one another only by reason of their belonging to the human species and of their concern for its perpetuation, but united not at all on the basis of their sharing a common spiritual world. Indeed, when the human community has become a kind of vast household in which the major activi-

71. W. H. Auden, "Thinking What We Are Doing," in *Encounter*, vol. 12, no. 6 (June 1959), p. 72.
72. Arendt, *The Human Condition*, p. 28.

ties are housekeeping activities calculated to guarantee the maintenance of life for the individual and the species; when (as in a family) there is no longer any distance between people, so that, instead of acting as individuals, they "play roles" and behave like robots; and when the conduct of this household's affairs is taken over by anonymous bureaucrats, so that the predominant form of government becomes that of "rule by nobody" (which may be "one of . . . [the] cruelest and most tyrannical versions"[73] of government)—when this is the reigning state of affairs (as Miss Arendt takes it to have been, with ever increasing inordinacy, over the past two hundred years), then, as she would say, the human world has fallen under the sway of "society," which is in its very essence a *mass* reality.

The bench mark in relation to which she takes her measure of the human City in our time is that which is for her represented by the Greek *polis* of the great Athenian age of the fifth century, the age of Pericles and Thucydides, of Plato and Isocrates. And, when she moves back from the drifting, muddled world of the present to that exemplary moment made by the Greek city-state, what she finds to be of greatest interest in that ancient mode of life was its containment of "society" within the realm of the private household. For the Greeks, as she maintains, conceived the home and the family to be the center of all the various forms of merely social companionship that may be necessary for the satisfaction of man's natural wants and needs. Here, in the realm of the household, the presiding figure was the *paterfamilias* who, in the style of an unchallengeable autocrat, so governed the family circle and its enslaved retainers as to provide for all the necessities of the domestic order and to sustain the ongoing processes of life: here it was, under the guardianship of the penates, that the man labored to provide nourishment for the individual and the woman labored (in giving birth) to provide for the survival of the species. And it was from out of the dim, sheltered interior of this nonpolitical (or prepolitical) realm of the household that a freeman stepped forth into the life of the City, into the world of "action," into that public space of the *politikos* where, by well-chosen words and courageous deeds,

73. Ibid., p. 40.

he joined his equals in the pursuit not of life but of "the good life."

In the context of the Greek city-state, as Miss Arendt insists, the household was the domain of necessity—where the slaves labored that their master might be liberated from all gross employments, where the woman labored to bring forth new life; and it was only in the public forums of the commonwealth that freedom dwelt, where men, having left the dark alcoves of the private region, moved among their equals to initiate common enterprises and to conduct the business of the *polis*. Here it was, indeed, in the world of the *politikos*, that, having been liberated from those necessities of nature served by the household, men could truly become individuals, as they embarked on important civic undertakings and (by their words and deeds) strove with one another for glory. Indeed, the whole *raison d'être* of politics was that of providing an unpolluted, invigorating public space in which, as they attended to the affairs of the City, men might so test one another as to discover whom it was who deserved to be admitted into the fellowship of the brave and the true. Which meant, of course, that the reality of the *polis* was something incommensurable with the range of meanings presided over by our modern concept of "ideology," for politics— namely, that enterprise which concerned the *polis*—was in no wise conceived to be any kind of superstructure of social and economic interests, since these touched not the life of the *polis* but belonged wholly to the private sphere of the household. Nor was politics an affair of rulership and legislation. True, a stable structure of law was required, for, apart from established ordinances, "a public realm could no more exist than a piece of property without a fence to hedge it in; the one harbored and inclosed political life as the other sheltered and protected the biological life process of the family."[74] But the making of laws was not the *content* of political action. And rulership had no place in the political sphere, since the *polis* knew only "equals" (*homoioi*) who neither commanded nor submitted to commands. Instead, what was of the essence of things in the public realm was not the administering of institutions or the enactment of laws

74. Ibid., p. 64.

or the policing of the rabble but rather the affiliation in great enterprise of men who, in fact only by acting together, found their freedom and thus came into their full human stature. "The public realm, in other words, was reserved for individuality; it was the only place where men could show who they really and inexchangeably were. It was for the sake of this chance, and out of love for a body politic that made it possible to them all, that each was more or less willing to share in the burden of jurisdiction, defense, and administration of public affairs."[75]

In the contemporary world, however, as Miss Arendt argues, the basic terms of the Greek situation are quite radically reversed. For, in our own time, "society" has invaded the public realm, so much so that this latter is now but the ancient household writ large. The despotic rule of the Greek *paterfamilias* has been replaced by the various impersonal machineries of our modern bureaucratic ethos, to be sure, but "rule by nobody" represents rulership, nevertheless, often of the most severely tyrannous kind. And what Hannah Arendt considers to be most decisively characteristic of the modern world is its way of gathering us together in the manner in which the members of a Greek household were constituted twenty-five hundred years ago. Just as, anciently, the private household was the realm where men were united towards the end of sustaining the life process, of providing for individual survival and the continuity of the species, so now the public realm, is, most essentially, a vast community of laborers and jobholders organized around activities necessary for the sustenance of life. And, just as the polity of the ancient household allowed no real room for individuality (which, for the freeman, was to find its expression *outside* the household, in the public realm of the *polis*), so, again, our own world, under the dominion now of "society," tends to accord the person a purely abstract and functional identity: he becomes merely a commodity in the marketplace, to be "packaged" in the manners and styles of behavior appropriate to his "role." In short, what Marx called the "socialization of man" has so completely transformed the public spaces of the modern age that, far from affording today the kind of environment for self-realization offered by the

75. Ibid., p. 41.

public realm of the Greek *polis,* they now represent precisely that from which men want to flee in their quest of the chance for a human life. "The emergence of society—the rise of house-keeping, its activities, problems, and organizational devices—from the shadowy interior of the household into the light of the public sphere, has not only blurred the old borderline be-tween private and political, it has also changed almost beyond recognition the meaning of the two terms and their significance for the life of the individual and the citizen."[76] For whereas, anciently, the "privacy" of the household did indeed represent a privative principle, when viewed over against the realm of the *polis* which was the sphere of freedom, today the opposite of privacy is not the world of the *politikos* but the realm of "society" which is something like a slave-economy, where men are identified merely by the functions they perform, where they are governed by the iron laws of conformity and "shuffled to-gether like grains of sand."[77] So, as a consequence, says Hannah Arendt, the private realm, far from being (as it. was in Greek antiquity) the realm of the not-yet-human, has become for us—opposed as it now is to the dominion of "society"—the sphere of intimacy. And thus it is a world no longer barren and unpro-pitious but rather one felt to be rich and manifold, offering the one remaining shelter against the mediocrity and confusion of mass-life, offering indeed the one region in which a man may hope to be free.

So great is Miss Arendt's sense of the fearful losses entailed by this whole development that she is noticeably reluctant to invite the conclusion that the private realm deserves now to be regarded as an important base for "political" action, for action intended to rehabilitate and to fortify the *polis.* True, she is not quite prepared to account "the modern discovery of inti-macy" as merely a flight from the discouragements of the public scene into the less daunting world of individual subjectivity. But "the consequences for human existence when both the public and private spheres of life are gone, the public because it has

76. Ibid., p. 38.
77. Karl Jaspers, *Man in the Modern Age,* trans. Eden and Cedar Paul (Garden City, N.Y.: Doubleday Anchor Books, 1957), p. 50.

become a function of the private and the private because it has become the only common concern left"[78]—the consequences of this whole chain of circumstances appear to her to be so expensive that she is not eager to push forward any consoling principle of compensation. Yet, after looking at essentially the same developments and issues that engaged Hannah Arendt, many of those over the past generation whom we think of as among the most thoughtful analysts of our condition—and people representing such diversity in fundamental viewpoint, say, as E. M. Forster and Martin Buber, George Orwell and Gabriel Marcel, Simone Weil and Ignazio Silone—have not hesitated to embrace the possibility that, now, at the end of the modern age, a politics looking toward the redemption of the City may need to be carried on, at least in part, within the regions of the personal life. In this connection it should not go unnoticed how careful Auden himself was, in his review of Miss Arendt's book, approvingly to remark her lesson, that "What a modern man thinks of as the realm where he is free to be himself and to disclose himself to others, is what he calls his private or personal life, that is to say, the nearest modern equivalent to the public realm of the Greeks is the intimate realm. . . ."[79] And, indeed, it is just in this range of thought, so masterfully charted by Hannah Arendt's *The Human Condition*, that we may locate the main ballast of the poetry of Auden's last years.

Throughout, of course, the whole stretch of his career he conceived the name and nature of the human world to be that of the City: which is to say that, early and late, he took it for granted that the primary fact of human existence is that we are members one of another. True, the particular cities of the world —those "Built by the conscience-stricken, the weapon-making,/ By us"—are often to be found "unlucky," "assaulted," and "starved." But, over a long period, their failure to be places "where/The will of love is done" only prompted Auden's poetry to bid us, again and again, to seek the Just City, to (as he said in *Look, Stranger!*) "rebuild our cities, not dream of islands." Yet, as his Page-Barbour Lectures at the University of Virginia

78. Arendt, *The Human Condition*, p. 69.
79. W. H. Auden, "Thinking What We Are Doing," p. 76.

(*The Enchafèd Flood*) indicate, he was already at the end of the 1940s beginning to be deeply troubled by the strange inexorability with which urban democracy in our time turns the individual "into a cypher of the crowd, or a mechanical cogwheel in an impersonal machine."[80]   And a decade later, no doubt largely helped by the influence of Hannah Arendt, he had become convinced of the disappearance altogether of the Public Realm as a sphere of authentically human life: as he said in one of the leading essays ("The Poet & the City") in *The Dyer's Hand,*

> To the Greeks the Private Realm was the sphere of life ruled by the necessity of sustaining life, and the Public Realm the sphere of freedom where a man could disclose himself to others. Today, the significance of the terms private and public has been reversed; public life is the necessary impersonal life, the place where a man fulfills his social function, and it is in his private life that he is free to be his personal self.[81]

Or, again, as it is said in the great poem "The Shield of Achilles" (after which his book of 1955 was entitled), now we dwell not in the "Marble well-governed cities" of the Greeks but on an unfeatured plain where there is "no sign of neighborhood," where "An unintelligible multitude"—"A million eyes, a million boots in line"—waits "for a sign," as ragged urchins loiter, as "girls are raped" and "two boys knife a third." "The mass and majesty of this world" have fallen into the hands of "bored officials" who give statistical proof that some cause is just to those who've "never heard/Of any world where promises were kept,/Or one could weep because another wept."   And in such a time, as Auden concluded, the heroic image is to be sought "neither [in] the 'Great Man' nor [in] the romantic rebel . . . but [in] the man or woman in any walk of life who, despite all the impersonal pressures of modern society, manages to acquire and preserve a face of his own."[82]

"When little was left standing/But the suburb of dissent," it

80. W. H. Auden, *The Enchafèd Flood, or The Romantic Iconography of the Sea* (New York: Random House, 1950), p. 27.
81. W. H. Auden, *The Dyer's Hand* (New York: Random House, 1962), p. 80.
82. Ibid., p. 84.

seemed necessary, then, to turn from "Metropolis, that too-great city," toward this remaining purlieu, in order there to explore the new "conditions [to which] we must bow/In building the Just City now." Auden's vision of this bordering region wherein one may learn anew "To serve mankind's *imperium*," though it was to be developed fully only in the series of books begun in 1965 with *About the House,* had already been beautifully pre-figured in *New Year Letter,* where, early on in Part III, amidst the festivities signalizing the arrival of the new year of 1940, he began all of a sudden directly to address Elizabeth Mayer, to whom the poem was dedicated:

> Warm in your house, Elizabeth,
> A week ago at the same hour
> I felt the unexpected power
> That drove our ragged egos in
> From the dead-ends of greed and sin
> To sit down at the wedding feast,
> Put shining garments on the least,
> Arranged us so that each and all,
> The erotic and the logical,
> Each felt the *placement* to be such
> That he was honoured overmuch,
> And Schubert sang and Mozart played
> And Gluck and food and friendship made
> Our privileged community
> That real republic which must be
> The State all politicians claim,
> Even the worst, to be their aim.

And it is, indeed, in such an excellent fellowship as this, in the generous civility that prevails in "the *polis* of our friends," that, as Auden came to feel, we may now find our best image of the true City and a kind of outpost from which to begin the work of renewing the ruined walls of "that too-great city," that "dread Leviathan," called Metropolis.

It is in the poems that he brought together in his book of the mid-sixties, *About the House*—and most especially in the long, beautiful sequence entitled "Thanksgiving for a Habitat"—that we get what is perhaps the decisive statement of the deeply chastened, yet wonderfully sunny, sobriety marking Auden's late maturity. In the late fifties he had bought a house in the little village of Kirchstetten in southern Austria, less than thirty miles out of Vienna and only ninety kilometers removed from "where minefield and watchtower say *No Exit*": what he had never dared hope for was, as he said (in *About the House*), at last, "in my fifties, mine, a toft-and-croft/where I needn't, ever, be at home *to*/those I am not at home *with*. . . ." And it is this rustic seat which the book of 1965 makes an image of the House, of those places of intimacy "haphazardly scattered over the earth" where men may meet "without papers"—to cultivate "authentic comity."

The great opening cycle of poems, in speaking their thanks for this Habitat, perform a little eucharist for each of its rooms. "The Cave of Making," which is an elegy for Louis MacNeice, speaks of the room—"more private than a bedroom even"—which was Auden's study, where (amongst Olivetti portable and heaps of paper and the very best dictionaries money could buy) he served that

> unpopular art which cannot be turned into
> background noise for study
> or hung as a status trophy by rising executives,
> cannot be "done" like Venice
> or abridged like Tolstoy, but stubbornly still insists upon
> being read or ignored. . . .

"Down There" is devoted to the "cellar underneath the house" which is very much unlike the other rooms, for, "When trunks are being packed, and when, without warning,/We drive up in the dark, unlock and switch lights on,/They seem put out" and wear an injured look—but the cellar, keeping in all seasons its wine and conserves and other good things ripened by the sun, "never takes umbrage": though visited only when its stores are needed, "It takes us as we are, explorers, homebodies. . . ."

"Up There" celebrates the attic which "no clock recalls . . . /Once an hour to the household it's a part of" and where all sorts of things—old letters and bulging boxes and galoshes—"Wait unworshipped."

"The Geography of the House" is devoted to the "white-tiled cabin" in which one sits at stool after breakfast, and the poem's parenthesis says:

(Orthodoxy ought to
Bless our modern plumbing:
Swift and St. Augustine
Lived in centuries,
When a stench of sewage
Ever in the nostrils
Made a strong debating
Point for Manichees.)

"Encomium Balnei" extols the one room in the house which "has only an inside lock," the room in which, lying snugly in hot water, one may "present a Lieder Abend/to a captive audience of . . . [one's] toes." "Grub First, Then Ethics" is devoted to the fine modern kitchen Auden had installed in the little Kirchstetten house, "For Friends Only" to the bedroom for guests, and "The Cave of Nakedness" to his own bedroom.

But, of all the poems taking us on this tour, it is perhaps "The Common Life," which is devoted to the living room, and, even more especially, "Tonight at Seven-Thirty" (whose setting is the dining room) which offer the fullest hints of what these parables are proposing. The six stanzas of the latter poem speak of a dinner-party at which six congenial guests are assembled, and six because in these days one's likely to find it necessary to be one's own "chef, servitor and scullion." The gathering is "small and unpublic," and, though a sparklingly festive occasion, a certain requisite formality is carefully kept, for this "is a worldly rite that nicknames or endearments/or family/diminutives would profane": to be the means of grace that it ought to be, a dinner-party must be informed by the virtues of deference and courtesy. And thus "two doters who wish/to tiddle and curmurr between the soup and fish/belong in restaurants." For those who come together around the board are there—if, as may be hoped, they have "stalwart digestions"—to enjoy the food, but also to enjoy one another and to talk to one another as wittily and courteously and attentively as they can:

a brawler may not
be put to death on the spot,
but he is asked to quit the sacral dining area
instanter, and a foul-mouth gets the cold
shoulder.

Nor does one want saints at table, and surely not a god, for

> he would be too odd
> to talk to and, despite his imposing presence, a bore,
> for the funniest
> mortals and the kindest are those who are most aware
> of the baffle of being, don't kid themselves our care
> is consolable, but believe a laugh is less
> heartless than tears, that a hostess
> prefers it.

What one hopes for, at seven-thirty of an evening, is six lenient, politic, graceful people amongst whom there is much "well-liking" and who are adept at keeping "the eye grateful/for what Nature's bounty and grace of Spirit can create"—

> men
> and women who enjoy the cloop of corks, appreciate
> depatical fare, yet can see in swallowing
> a sign act of reverence,
> in speech a work of re-presenting
> the true olamic silence.

What the poem conjures up, in short, is a microcosm of that more spacious Coinherence which the *civitas terrena* was meant to be, an image of that hither side of "the demanded *caritas*"[83] which is not "glory" but thoughtful generosity and "civility": the little banquet that the poem arranges intends, in other words, to be but a small simulacrum of the civic world to which we are summoned in all the larger relations of life.

And it is a similar image that "The Common Life" wants to invoke. The poem is dedicated to Chester Kallman, with whom Auden shared his life over many years, and it cannot resist marveling at how each has managed to forgive in the other "impossible behavior,/to endure by some miracle/conversational tics and larval habits/without wincing," and at how they have thus created "a common world/between them":

> It's a wonder that neither
> has been butchered by accident,
>
> or, as lots have, silently vanished into
> History's criminal noise

83. Charles Williams, *He Came Down from Heaven* (London: Faber and Faber, 1940), p. 96.

> unmourned for, but that, after twenty-four years,
>   we should sit here in Austria
> as cater-cousins, under the glassy look
>   of a Naples Bambino,
> the portrayed regards of Strauss and Stravinsky,
>   doing British crossword puzzles,
> is very odd indeed.

Yet the poem is not all marveling, for, as it contemplates that "catholic area" of the living room which each is free to "enter/ without knocking, leave without a bow," and where "There's no *We* at an instant,/only *Thou* and *I*," it suggests that, in not having carelessly flung themselves upon each other and in having prudently chosen not to trespass upon each other's solitude, the real secret of this "common life" which they have built together lies in its having been so ordered as to allow for "two regions/ of protestant being which nowhere overlap." And thus we are given another parable of what the modern City would be like, if it were what "The Cave of Nakedness" calls a "Country of Consideration."

So the statement being made in "Thanksgiving for a Habitat" (as in many of the other poems in *About the House*), far from representing any sort of "apoliticalism," expresses a profoundly *political* concern. The careless, or the shortsighted, reader may quickly conclude that this celebrant of a merely domestic *polis* was one who, unfortunately, had been driven by the adversities of the age into the special kind of amnesia suffered by the thoroughly privatized man. And one or another version of this judgment has been rendered with tiresome regularity over the past decade or so by various and sundry professors and reviewers for liberal weeklies and Sunday supplement hacks. But what is too much disregarded in the quasi-official view of the presumed *trahison* represented by Auden's late phase is precisely his own conviction that the Private Realm has in our time become what the Public Realm anciently was—namely, the place in which a truly human language is spoken and in which men by their words and deeds may disclose themselves to one another with forthrightness and candor. In the Great World of our period, in what political economists call "the public sector," as Auden felt—and he was surely not mistaken—we have in effect come to what Daniel Bell some years ago was declaring to be "the end of ideology."[84] Though Auden himself never made use of Mr. Bell's phrase, it does very exactly render his general sense of the modern landscape. For, with a splendidly commonsensical kind of clarity, he saw that *out there*, in the Great World, no real debate any longer goes on, since capitalism and socialism and communism are all seeking essentially the same goal: which is to say, as he defined the matter, that they are all seeking "to guarantee to every member of society, as a psychophysical organism, the right to physical and mental health."[85] But such a goal, he believed—as a thinker like Hannah Arendt would also contend—is hardly a *political* goal, since, as he said, "it is not concerned with human beings as persons and citizens but with human bodies, with the precultural, prepolitical human creature."[86] Politics, in other words—or that field of activity having to do with men's distinctively human relations with one another—concerns, most principally, not the basic necessities of life, not the issues that fell under the superintendence of the ancient household, but that level of the human enterprise related to the dimension of freedom. So when in fact the Public Realm has become the sphere of what Hannah Arendt calls "action," it is, as Auden expected us to realize, to be supremely *political*—and supremely committed to the renovation of "the public sector"—to focus in on that area of the world where men can still be men: to wit, the department of life which for the ancients was opposed to the *polis* but which is *for us* the very center of the *polis*, namely, the sphere of intimacy, where a climate still prevails in which "regions of protestant being" may freely meet.

In his last years, then, though long since having forsworn any kind of Agit-Prop, he remained a poet under conscription to the City, but wanting—in his "suburb of dissent"—very greatly to deepen our contemporary conception of what it means to be a politically engaged man, wanting indeed (as Lionel Trilling

84. See Daniel Bell, *The End of Ideology* (New York: Collier Books, 1961).
85. W. H. Auden, *The Dyer's Hand*, p. 87.
86. Ibid.

already in the mid-1940s was urging us to do) "to force [back]
into our definition of politics every human activity and every
subtlety of every human activity."[87]   "There are," said Mr.
Trilling, "manifest dangers in doing this, but greater dangers in
not doing it.   Unless we insist that politics is imagination and
mind, we will learn"—as Auden might have said, from the Managers—"that imagination and mind are politics, and of a kind
that we will not like."[88]   And, in all the wonderfully complex
and graceful pirouettes that this poet of the Loyal Opposition
was making his language perform in the work of the closing
years of his career, he was attempting, over and above the
"argument" he advanced, to execute a political gesture, to present what he hoped might be an invigorating model of the punctiliousness and *esprit* with which a man ought to undertake to
talk to other men.   He wanted, in short, not only to rehabilitate
politics (in its classical sense), and this for the sake of the City,
but also to make us remember again that a truly human politics
is imagination and mind, in their fullest and most consequential
intensity.   The concluding passage of "Thanksgiving for a
Habitat" (the title-poem in the sequence), after speaking of the
Kirchstetten house as a place where one needn't be at home *to*
those one isn't at home *with*, says that it is "not a cradle,/ . . .
and not a windowless grave, but a place/I may go both in and
out of."   And so it is, with that miniature *civitas* of Auden's
Private Realm which is located in a suburban precinct: it is a
place one goes out of again and again into the Great World,
there to treat with Caesar's minions and to serve, as best one
can, "mankind's *imperium.*"

The final books—*City without Walls, Epistle to a Godson,*
and *Thank You, Fog*—though they contain many impressive
declarations of this great old Horatian, do not add any new
dimension to the funded testimony of the period initiated by
Nones.   It is a quiet, gentle, conversational speech we hear, of
one who does not now intend (as François Duchene puts it) "to

87. Lionel Trilling, *The Liberal Imagination* (New York: Viking Press,
1950), p. 100.
88. Ibid.

be entangled in youth's false airs and graces"[89]—though, as he says in the dedicatory lines in *Epistle to a Godson*, "at Twenty I tried to/vex my elders, past Sixty it's the young whom I hope to bother."

Auden liked to think of Ariel as the genius of poetic *divertissement* and of Prospero as the tutelary of poetry in its sapient mode, and both, together, would seem to be presiding over the last poems. A quite typical instance of the characteristic manner and tone (when any large subject is being approached) is presented by the opening poem in *City without Walls*. Here, three voices are heard, and it is the first, with its savage account of the contemporary scene, which speaks at greatest length. It says:

> "Those fantastic forms, fang-sharp,
> bone-bare, that in Byzantine painting
> were a shorthand for the Unbounded
> beyond the Pale, unpolicied spaces
> where dragons dwelt and demons roamed
>
> "colonized only by ex-worldlings,
> penitent sophists and sodomites,
> are visual facts in the foreground now,
> real structures of steel and glass:
> hermits, perforce, are all today. . . ."

And this first voice goes on to speak of how, in this "Gadgeted Age" of "Hobbesian Man . . . mass-produced," "all has gone phut"—of how we dwell now in the lawless marches of Asphalt Lands, "where gangs clash and cops turn/robber barons"; of how

> "Every workday Eve fares
> forth to the stores her foods to pluck,
> while Adam hunts an easy dollar:
> unperspiring at eventide
> both eat their bread in boredom of spirit.
>
> "The weekend comes that once was holy,
> free still, but a feast no longer,
> just time out, idiorhythmic,
> when no one cares what his neighbor does:
> now newsprint and network are needed most. . . ."

89. François Duchene, *The Case of the Helmeted Airman*, p. 165.

Indeed, in stanza after stanza, this first voice is to be heard dryly marshaling the various signs and evidences of the stunted-ness and vacancy that prevail in the False or the Unreal City of this late, bad time—till finally the voice is broken off by Auden's saying, "Thus I was thinking at three a.m./in mid-Manhattan. . . ." Then, as he says, these musings were suddenly "cut short" by another voice, "a sharp voice":

> "What fun and games you find it to play
> Jeremiah-cum-Juvenal:
> Shame on you for your *Schadenfreude*."

And, at the end, the irony is redoubled, as the poet's debate with the second voice is interrupted by a third voice:

> "My!" I blustered, "how moral we're getting.
> A pococurante?   Suppose I were,
> so what, if my words are true."

> Thereupon, bored, a third voice:
> "Go to sleep now for God's sake!
> You both will feel better by breakfast time."

Now it is just such a steady, affable equanimity as this that gives to the final poems their special kind of charm. The man who is speaking to us is one by no means forgetful that "never as yet/has Earth been without/her bad patch, some unplace with/jobs for torturers"—and he does not fail to remark "how glib all the faces I see about me/seem . . . to have become." "Housman was perfectly right./Our world rapidly worsens:/nothing now is so horrid/or silly it can't occur." But, as he says to himself, "Why . . . should I badger?" "No rheum has altered my gait, as ever my cardiac muscles/ are undismayed, my cells/perfectly competent": so, despite his frequently hinted confidence that death was not far off, he wanted to live *gratefully*, to view all that had been granted by Dame Kind eucharistically, to make his days (in the great old phrase of the Anglican Prayerbook's anaphora) a "sacrifice of praise and thanksgiving." And thus he beautifully toasts old friends—Nevill Coghill, Marianne Moore, William Empson, physicians who've treated him, the remarkable old peasant who was his housekeeper in Kirchstetten for ten years; he prepares an "Epistle" to his godson, Philip Spender (bidding him on the Quest Perilous to keep his toes turned out as he walks and to remember he's a Spender), and an "Epithalamium" for Peter Mudford and Rita Auden; in syllabic meters and alliterative structures of extraordinary refinement he, in numerous occasional poems, explores the ordinary fears and embarrassments that beset most of us, those who are not amongst "the top intelligent few"; he produces wonderfully turned out little *haiku* which write various kinds of marginalia on the great central themes of his work; he now and again, after talking to Goethe and to dogs and mice and *contra* Blake, talks directly to himself—

> Time, we both know, will decay You, and already
> I'm scared of our divorce: I've seen some horrid ones.
> Remember: when *Le Bon Dieu* says to You *Leave him!*,
> please, please, for His sake and mine, pay no attention
> to my piteous *Dont's*, but bugger off quickly.

And always the background against which these last poems are written is that garrisoned *civitas* of the Private Realm, whose goodly fellowship of faithful friends and true neighbors, as Auden says in *Epistle to a Godson* ("The Garrison"), is intended by his poetic designs "to serve as a paradigm/now of what a plausible Future might be"—of that future in which "the story/ Of our human city" would

> move
> Like music when,
> Begotten notes
> New notes beget,
> Making the flowing
> Of time a growing,
> Till what it could be
> At last it is,
> Where even sadness
> Is a form of gladness,
> Where Fate is Freedom,
> Grace and Surprise.

It must be apparent, then, even to his most cursory readers, that those modern theorists who claim that the poet does in no way supervise any kind of truly propositional discourse would be ill advised to seek evidentiary support of their position in the poetry of Auden. For, from beginning to end, it is a poetry untouched by any skepticism about its own capacity to handle systematic ideas, and is deeply committed to its chosen task of bearing "witness to the truth." If something like this were being said in a university classroom, the force of the conventions prevailing there would doubtless prompt one's students to make an act of obeisance to the pieties of the graduate school by demanding that careful notice be taken of the ways in which Auden's various "forms" *establish* his meanings. And, faced with such a demand, one would not in desperation be driven back against the blackboard, since, given his profound integrity of "vision" and given a virtuosity of craftsmanship unrivaled in the modern period by anyone other than Yeats, Auden's work presents one of the great examples in the poetry of our time of " 'unified' utterance."[90] But, after the requisite responses had been made in a university seminar to the demand for certification of unity of "form" and "content," the fact would still stand that Auden's is a poetry wanting, in very nearly a forensic sense, to be *heard*, wanting its drift and purport to be tried and appraised. And thus—particularly with the late poems whose emphasis so collides with many of our most deeply settled presumptions—we cannot finally evade that question which academic literary scholasticism generally considers it gauche for critical discourse to undertake to confront in a simple and direct way: namely, may the deliverances of this poet be conceived to be in any sense true?

We, of course—or, let us say, most of the people who make themselves heard in the public forums of our period—take it for granted that the Just City is chiefly served by those who circulate petitions and join picket lines, who attend boring meetings and who distribute equally boring pamphlets, who treat with the agents of sectarian conclaves and who engage in the choreography of "confrontation" politics. And such a testimony as comes out of Auden's last years—about the spheres of life in which we may find our clearest paradigms of the "plausible Future"—will doubtless seem to many to entail nothing other than an advo-

90. The phrase is Gerald Graff's: see his *Poetic Statement and Critical Dogma* (Evanston: Northwestern University Press, 1970), chap. Six.

157

cacy, while Rome burns, of a virtual abdication from the historical arena. It will perhaps be acknowledged that he was not, to
be sure, a patron of those young Gnostics who have recently
espoused everyone's doing his own "thing," but, as some may
impatiently insist, there is no large final difference between the
individualistic antinomianism promoted by the new Bohemia
and this retreat (however precautious) from the jungles of
Metropolis into "the *polis* of our friends"—differences in cultural
tone, yes, as between the puerile crudity of the one and the
assured urbanity of the other, but no final difference as regards
the essential substance of what is held forth as a program for
life.

Yet it may be just here, in the supposition that the Auden of
Nones and *About the House* and *City without Walls* is primarily
committed to the espousal of a kind of program (which says,
Back to the catacombs—or the barracks, or the cottages)—it
may be just here, in this supposition, that a primary mistake is
made. Auden did, of course, believe that people dwelling
amidst disorder in their private lives are not likely, in the larger
relations of their social business, to fashion anything good and
humane, and he also felt that to have kept peace in one's own
household is, therefore, to have contributed to the well-being of
one's community, to have offered to one's compatriots a sign and
pledge of what James Joyce called "the fair courts of life." But
he was not a sentimental fool, and he was never for a moment
by way of supposing that the affairs of the Great World will
somehow take care of themselves, if the *honnête homme* simply
keeps his hearth. Yet he did want steadily to keep his eye on
what is often well-nigh forgotten by the fashionable forms of
contemporary seriousness—namely, that the real goal of all the
petitions and boring meetings and picket lines is not merely
more petitions and more picket lines but what Shakespeare's
Ferdinand speaks of in *The Tempest* as "quiet days, fair issue,
and long life." He knew, as we have noticed he was also careful to say, that the House—or the realm where one abides with
family and friends and neighbors—is a place one both goes in
and *out* of; but all that we do *out there*, in our efforts to promote
shalom in the City, is done in order that there might be peace

and blessedness in those precincts where boys and girls fall in love and children are born and the old and the young peer at family albums by lamplight. Which is to say that in the plausible future, in the world of the Just City, men will not be straining after some new stratagem in the politics of "confrontation" but will, as we ought surely to hope, be at ease—taking their Sunday baths, tooting at neighbors across the backyard fence, reading Colette, marveling at Balanchine, and at martini-time drawing the curtains and choosing a composer they would like to hear before sitting down with friends at table before some good savory mess.[91] And it is of these "fair courts" that Auden's late poems want to bring news: they are, in other words, poems stirred by "the old vision of the noble life,"[92] and they are deeply informed by the conviction that "the norm [for the human City] . . . is one of order, peace, honour, and beauty"[93]—which is a vision of the world that, finally, will be declared *untrue* perhaps only by "the possessed," by those who take the ideal human condition to be one in which things are being wrenched apart and broken up and brought to an end.

Auden was one, however, who most stringently disavowed all the various forms of Gnostic contempt for Creation, since he had been taught by the Christian faith and by his own experience to conceive the world as everywhere filled with rumors of angels and touched with Glory. As he said in the final lines of "Whitsunday in Kirchstetten" (*About the House*),

> about
> catastrophe or how to behave in one
> I know nothing, except what everyone knows—
> if there when Grace dances, I should dance.

---

91. The concluding figure in the sentence above draws on Auden's "The Garrison" (in *Epistle to a Godson*). And, in this sentence, a portion of what precedes the concluding figure represents a raiding of a fine passage in Irving Howe's essay on "The City in Literature," where, after having brilliantly reviewed the kind of animus toward the city carried by much of modern literature, he asks finally what it is, indeed, that we may be expected to do in the *Just* City—to which he answers: "Take our Sunday baths. . . ." See his *The Critical Point* (New York: Horizon Press, 1973), p. 58.

92. See Lionel Trilling, *Sincerity and Authenticity* (Cambridge: Harvard University Press, 1972), chap. II.

93. Ibid., p. 39.

The *Benedicite* of the Church's Morning Office bids the sun and the moon, the showers and the dews, the frost and the cold, the fowls of the air and all green things on earth, the mountains and hills, and all the children of men to "bless the Lord," to "praise him, and magnify him for ever." And it was in this spirit, of Catholic obedience, that he made that great declaration in *Nones*—

> I could (which you cannot)
> Find reasons fast enough
> To face the sky and roar
> In anger and despair
> At what is going on,
> Demanding that it name
> Whoever is to blame:
> The sky would only wait
> Till all my breath was gone
> And then reiterate
> As if I wasn't there
> That singular command
> I do not understand,
> *Bless what there is for being,*
> Which has to be obeyed, for
> What else am I made for,
> Agreeing or disagreeing.

It is, indeed, with an iteration of this doxology—"Bless what there is for being"—that an account of Auden's service as a poet to the City ought to close, since what was so much of the essence of his faith and thought was the certainty that, when the relations of life that give substance and graciousness to the City are dismantled, we shall be rescued from the *Blick ins Chaos* only by a supernatural love. And so eloquently did he bear witness to this belief that, as he went about his work of disclosing "some of the room still left on a sadly crowded planet in which human freedom might grow,"[94] we—even in a secular age—felt him to be, after Eliot's death, beyond doubt the great poet of the age.

94. Hollander, "Auden at Sixty," p. 87.

Bibliographical Notes and Acknowledgments

The chapter on T. S. Eliot was originally published in the *Journal of the American Academy of Religion* (vol. 42, no. 2, June 1974) under the title "Eliot and the Orphic Way." And the chapter on W. H. Auden incorporates a few passages from an essay published in the *Chicago Review* (vol. 13, no. 4, Winter 1959) under the title "The Poetry of Auden." My thanks are herewith tendered to the editors of both journals for the permissions which they have kindly given for the reissuance of these materials in this book.

For permission to use quotations from copyrighted material the author is indebted to the following publishers: Random House—for passages from W. H. Auden's *Collected Longer Poems, The Age of Anxiety, Collected Shorter Poems, 1927–1957, Epistle to a Godson and Other Poems, The Dyer's Hand, City without Walls and Other Poems,* and *About the House,* and also for passages from André Malraux's *Man's Fate* (translated by Haakon M. Chevalier), *Days of Wrath* (translated by Haakon M. Chevalier), and *Man's Hope* (translated by Stuart Gilbert and Alastair MacDonald); the Viking Press—for a passage from W. H. Auden's Introduction to the *Portable Greek Reader,* and for a passage from his Introduction to *Poets of the English Language,* vol. 5 (edited by W. H. Auden and Norman Holmes Pearson); Harcourt Brace Jovanovich, Inc.—for passages from T. S. Eliot's *The Idea of a Christian Society, Four Quartets, Collected Poems 1909–1935,* and a passage from W. H. Auden's essay, "Squares and Oblongs," in *Poets at Work,* edited by C. D. Abbott; Alfred A. Knopf, Inc.—for a passage from "The Man with the Blue Guitar" in *The Collected Poems of Wallace Stevens*; William B. Eerdmans Publishing Co.—for a passage from Charles Williams's *Descent into Hell*; and Éditions Gallimard—for passages from André Malraux's *The Walnut Trees of Altenburg.*

The author is also indebted to Professor Edward Mendelson of Yale University, W. H. Auden's executor, for permission to quote a passage from Auden's poem "Petition."

Index

Index

Montale, Eugenio, 14
Montherlant, Henry de, 74
Moore, Marianne, 155
More, Sir Thomas, 24
Musil, Robert, viii

Nerval, Gérard de, 12
Niebuhr, H. Richard, 38n., 42
Niebuhr, Reinhold, 27, 113, 122, 140
Nietzsche, Friedrich, 53, 113
Novalis, 9, 11, 12

Ohmann, Richard M., 136n.
Ortega y Gasset, José, 40, 41n., 137
Orwell, George, 110, 145
Ott, Heinrich, 4
Ovid, 9
Owen, Wilfred, 109

Pascal, Blaise, 72, 96, 97, 113, 122
Pasternak, Boris, 48
Pericles, 141
Perse, St.-John, 9, 130
Pettazzoni, Raffaele, 16
Plato, 141
Polanyi, Michael, 17n.
Pound, Ezra, 17

Rahv, Philip, 29
Read, Herbert, 105
Replogle, Justin, 134
Righter, William, 51n.
Rilke, Rainer Maria, ix, 1, 7, 9, 12, 14, 17, 101–2, 104
Rimbaud, Arthur, 12, 103, 113
Robinson, James M., 4n.
Robinson, John A. T., 2n., 3
Rosenstock-Huessy, Eugen, 15
Rosenzweig, Franz, 15
Rougemont, Denis de, 140
Rousseau, Jean-Jacques, 40

Sartre, Jean-Paul, 40
Scheler, Max, 44
Schopenhauer, Arthur, 66
Scott, Nathan A., Jr., 4n., 35n.
Shelley, Percy Bysshe, vii, 11
Silone, Ignazio, 39, 47, 49, 145

Simmel, Georg, 137
Smith, Adam, 114
Smith, Ronald Gregor, 35
Spencer, Herbert, 114
Spender, Stephen, 12, 105, 121, 122
Spengler, Oswald, 53, 91
Spinoza, Baruch, 113
Stalin, Joseph, 140
Steiner, George, x
Stendhal, 97
Stéphane, Roger, 72
Stevens, Wallace, 2n., 4n., 13, 17, 101, 103, 104
Strauss, Walter A., 9, 10, 12, 13
Suarès, Guy, 97
Sun, Yat-sen, 57
Symanowski, Horst, 34, 35

Temple, William, 38
Thucydides, 141
Tillich, Paul, 113, 122
Trilling, Lionel, 35, 153, 159n.

Unamuno, Miguel de, 80

Valéry, Paul, 9, 17, 103
Van der Leeuw, Gerardus, 16
Vigny, Alfred Victor de, 97
Voltaire, François Marie Arouet de, 97, 110, 113

Wach, Joachim, 16
Wagner, Richard, 113
Watts, Isaac, 25
Weber, Max, 137
Weil, Simone, 145
Whitehead, Alfred North, 15n.
Whitman, Walt, 13
Wilder, Amos N., 3
Williams, Charles, x, 39n., 41n., 44–46, 95, 122, 140, 150n.
Williams, Raymond, vii, 48
Williams, William Carlos, xi, 39
Wordsworth, William, 10, 11, 13, 114

Yeats, William Butler, 13, 17, 39, 138, 157